Living Places

Living Places

Archaeology, Continuity and
Change at Historic Monuments
in Northern Ireland

by COLM J DONNELLY

THE INSTITUTE OF IRISH STUDIES
THE QUEEN'S UNIVERSITY OF BELFAST

This publication was commissioned
by the Cultural Traditions Group of the
Community Relations Council
for Northern Ireland

For my parents, Seamus and Rosaleen

Published 1997
Institute of Irish Studies
The Queen's University of Belfast

ISBN 0 85389 475 2

Printed by W&G Baird Ltd, Antrim
Designed by Rodney Miller Associates, Belfast

CONTENTS

ACKNOWLEDGEMENTS

The author carried out initial research on this book as a Junior Research Fellow at the Institute of Irish Studies, the Queen's University of Belfast. The Fellowship was sponsored by the Cultural Traditions Group of the Community Relations Council for Northern Ireland. I would like to thank Professor Brian Walker and my associate Fellows for making my stay at the Institute both educational and enjoyable, and Dr Maurna Crozier, of the Cultural Traditions Group, for her support and encouragement throughout the duration of my task. The Faculty of Arts in the Queen's University of Belfast and my postgraduate supervisor Dr Tom McNeill are both to be thanked for permitting me to suspend my PhD studies at the Department of Archaeology and Palaeoecology, the School of Geosciences, so that I might undertake the project. I would also like to thank my current employers, the Belcoo and District Development Group Ltd (and especially Ms Margaret Gallagher MBE), for all their support during the completion of the book.

My editor throughout the project has been Dr Ann Hamlin, Director of Built Heritage, DOE NI Environment and Heritage Service. With great patience she endured muddled drafts and innumerable queries, and she provided sterling guidance through the more problematic sections of the text. Her overall contribution to this work has been immense, none more so than where her own specialist knowledge of ecclesiastical monuments had to be called upon.

I would also like to thank Mr Nick Brannon, Professor Ronnie Buchanan, Dr Maurna Crozier, Mr Bobby Dickinson, Mr Barrie Hartwell, Ms Marion Meek, Mrs Margaret McNulty and Professor Brian Walker for reading over the completed text and providing many helpful comments and editorial advice. I must also express my gratitude to Ms Fiona Murray at the Community Relations Council for all her administrative assistance. The Cultural Traditions Group lent a portable computer during the initial stages of the project and I am indebted to Dr James Hawthorne for his technical assistance.

I received valuable advice and criticism from a number of individuals during the writing of certain sections of the text: Professor Mike Baillie (Dendrochronology), Mr Cormac Bourke (The Vikings), Mr Colin Breen (Underwater archae-ology), Mr Tony Cavanan (Townlands), Mr Barrie Hartwell (The Giant's Ring), Ms Claire Foley and Mr Declan Hurl (Inch Abbey), Dr Chris Lynn (Navan Fort and The Dorsey), Dr Jim Mallory (The Celts), Ms Eileen Murphy (Human and animal bone studies), Dr Gerry McCormac (Radiocarbon dating), Dr Tom McNeill (John de Courcy), Professor Jonathan Pilcher and Dr Valerie Hall (Beaghmore and Drumskinny), Mr Richard Warner (Lough na Cranagh) and Dr David Weir (Pollen analysis).

I would also like to thank Dr Kay Muhr (Department of Celtic, School of Medieval and Modern Languages, the Queen's University of Belfast) for all her advice on linguistic matters and for contributing Feature 15, a guide to the pronunciation of the Irish words included in the text.

Ms Gail Pollock, DOE NI Environment and Heritage Service, provided much help in the selection and copying of prints from the photographic record in Hill Street. I would also like to thank the same organisation for allowing me access to their photographic collection and permission to use their photographs and reconstructions in this book. The black and white infra-red photographs for each chapter title page are the work of Mr Tony Corey, DOE NI Environment and Heritage Service, and I wish to extend my appreciation for his permission to use these pieces of artwork in the book. Professor Mike Baillie, Mr Colin Breen, Mr Barrie Hartwell, Ms Eileen Murphy, Dr Gerry McCormac and Dr David Weir provided me with illustrations from their own collections, while Mr Cormac Bourke gave assistance and advice in selecting illustrations for The Celts and The Vikings. I would also like to thank Dr Michael Avery for permission to use his computer-generated distribution maps. The Ulster Museum, the Ulster History Park, the Ulster Folk and Transport Museum, the Public Records Office for Northern Ireland, the National Library of Ireland and the National Maritime Museum all provided me with photographs, and I am very grateful for all their co-operation and assistance.

This book has received support from the Cultural Traditions Programme of the Community Relations Council, which aims to encourage acceptance and understanding of cultural diversity in Northern Ireland.

ILLUSTRATIONS

Figures are numbered continuously. Unless otherwise indicated, all figures are Crown Copyright Reserved and reproduced with the permission of the Controller of Her Majesty's Stationery Office.

FRONT COVER: St Mary's Priory and mid 15th-century cross, Devenish, Co Fermanagh.
BACK COVER: Passage tomb at the Giant's Ring, Co Down.
FRONTISPIECE: Kilclief Castle, Co Down (Infra-red photograph by Tony Corey).

Figure

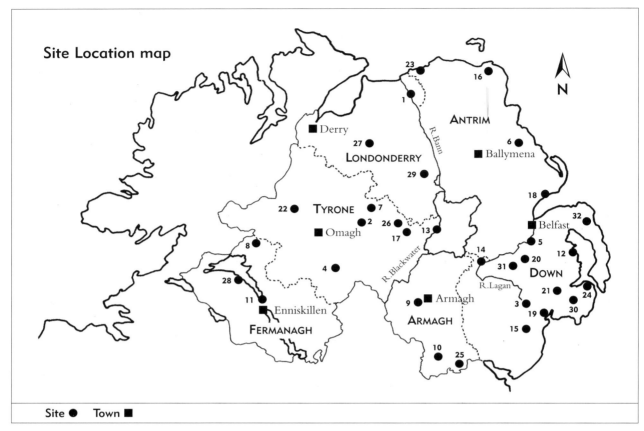

Site ● Town ■

1. Mount Sandel	9. Navan Fort	17. Tullaghoge	25. Moyry Castle
2. Creggandevesky	10. The Dorsey	18. Carrickfergus Castle	26. Derryloran Old Church
3. Legananny	11. Devenish	19. Dundrum Castle	27. Dungiven Priory
4. Knockmany	12. Nendrum	20. Duneight	28. Tully Castle
5. The Giant's Ring	13. Ardboe	21. Inch Abbey	29. Bellaghy Bawn
6. Dunteige	14. Rough Fort, Risk	22. Harry Avery's Castle	30. Struell Wells
7. Beaghmore	15. Drumena	23. Dunluce Castle	31. Hillsborough Fort
8. Drumskinny	16. Lough na Cranagh	24. Audley's Castle	32. Ballycopeland Windmill

ABBREVIATIONS

Co	County	*Ulster J Archaeol*	*Ulster Journal of Archaeology*
DOE NI	Department of the Environment for Northern Ireland	*JRSAI*	*Journal of the Royal Society of Antiquaries of Ireland*
ed	edited by	*PRIA*	*Proceedings of the Royal Irish Academy*
HMSO	Her Majesty's Stationery Office		
km	kilometre		
m	metre		

Preface

by CW Dickinson
Vice-President Ulster Archaeological Society

The Ulster Archaeological Society has a long and complicated history, going back to the 1850s, but it has a very clear objective – to further in every way the study of the past, particularly of Ulster. The Society aims to extend its outreach through lectures, outings and publications, especially through the *Ulster Journal of Archaeology*.

In 1991, therefore, when we heard about the Cultural Traditions Fellowship scheme we saw an opportunity to sponsor a Fellow and encourage the production of a popular, accessible book which would draw attention to the rich, many-stranded cultural heritage represented by our ancient monuments and buildings. As President of the Society at that time I applied to the Community Relations Council in February 1991 and Colm Donnelly was appointed to work for one year from September 1991 at the Queen's University Institute of Irish Studies, under the guidance of our committee member Dr Ann Hamlin.

The book's aim is to take the reader on a 'tour' of Northern Ireland's prehistory and history by considering a selection of monuments and buildings which, in different ways, illustrate the linked themes of continuity and change. We sincerely hope the book will advance the Ulster Archaeological Society's objective and appeal to a wide readership including teachers and others involved in education.

The Society is grateful to the Cultural Traditions Group for supporting the project and to the Institute of Irish Studies where the Fellowship was based. Thanks are also due to the Department of the Environment's Historic Monuments and Buildings Branch (now the Environment and Heritage Service) for much practical help with advice, information and illustrations. The Society's greatest debt, however, is to Dr Colm Donnelly who, over six years and with great dedication, has brought the book to completion. The Society is very pleased to have been associated with the book and we wish it well.

Fig. 1 Dunluce Castle, Co Antrim (Infra-red photograph by Tony Corey).

Chapter 1

Introduction

Northern Ireland is well known for the diversity of its landscape – from the lakes and islands of Fermanagh to the coastal splendour of Antrim and Londonderry, from the bleak bogs of Tyrone to the green drumlins of Down and Armagh. Historic monuments can be seen throughout this landscape, each one a record of past human activity in a locality and each containing a wealth of information on how our ancestors lived. This book is intended to examine the variety, richness and chronological depth of our historic monuments by looking at 32 carefully selected sites. It is hoped that readers will be encouraged to visit the monuments described in the book and similar monuments on their own doorsteps.

As the chosen subtitle suggests, two themes have been pursued throughout this book: 'continuity' and 'change'. The landscape is marked by the traces of past human activity, and while there is continuity in the use of the land from one generation to the next, there are also periods of change when new structures are added to modify or replace those of earlier inhabitants. We add our marks to the landscape in the form of buildings and agricultural or industrial activity before passing the land on to future generations who, in turn, will make their own contribution to the landscape. As a result of this process, evidence for many phases of activity accumulates in the landscape, with the ruined dwelling-places, mines or field systems of one generation superimposed on those of earlier generations.

At the historic monuments described in this book periods of change can be readily identified. The first major change to the landscape is the construction of what becomes today's historic monument. This may have a short life, becoming abandoned or forgotten or being replaced by those of later generations. It may, on the other hand, continue in use from one generation to the next, with each generation adding its own new elements to the structure. At some sites the two themes of continuity and change can be easily traced – Navan Fort or Carrickfergus Castle, for example. In other places a site was abandoned but a later building or feature was constructed near to it, as with the construction of Hillsborough Fort over an Early Christian rath. In the case of some church sites, like Devenish or Derryloran, continuity of ecclesiastical use can be established over a thousand years.

Two examples are offered here to illustrate these themes, neither included in the main text but discussed at this point to emphasise that the themes are traceable at sites other than the 32 cases included in the main text of the book. A drive through town or countryside will show the two processes in action today: the replacement of an old farmhouse with a bungalow, the extention of a graveyard into a neighbouring field, the demolition of a block of flats to make way for a new housing development – all these illustrate the themes of continuity and change. Our first example is the peaceful churchyard at Maghera, near Newcastle, Co Down (J 372341). The stump of a round tower marks the site of an early monastery founded in the 6th century AD. In the oval graveyard nearby stand the ruins of a medieval church and to the west of this stands the modern Church of Ireland church. The continuity in

Fig. 2 Maghera Old Church, Co Down.

the use of this site for worship since Early Christian times is clear from the remains still visible in the landscape. We move to the north coast for our second example, the small, late medieval stone castle at Dunseverick, Co Antrim (C 987446). The fragmentary tower stands on a basalt stack surrounded on three sides by the ocean. This castle, however, does not represent the first occupation on this promontory; its obvious defensive strength attracted settlement in pre-Norman times and *Dún Sobhairce* is mentioned in the Early Irish legends as well as historical annals.

It is the task of archaeologists to unravel this series of superimposed patterns and to build up a coherent story of the past. One way to do this is to study field monuments, earthworks and buildings – the visible heritage. A number of the sites in this book have also been investigated by excavation which allows us to look at the evidence that lies buried under the ground – the hidden heritage. By combining the information from both the

visible and invisible heritage the archaeologist builds up a picture of the history of a site and other sites of similar type: its origins, how it was built, why it was built, when it was built and when it was abandoned. With this information the archaeologist can then attempt to answer questions about lifestyle in the past, for it is with human history that they are ultimately concerned.

The origin of such investigation lies with the antiquarians of the last century – clerics, school teachers and other interested individuals who went from site to site recording the monuments and carrying out excavations. Their work could be prolific; it is estimated that one antiquarian working in Munster, Thomas J Westropp, published some 350 academic pieces during his lifetime. As interest in the past became more and more specialised the antiquarian tradition declined, though individuals such as the late William Stewart or the late Hugh A Boyd have shown the major role that local historians contribute to regional studies through their expert knowledge of the

Fig. 3 Dunseverick Castle, Co Antrim.

area where they live. Today in Northern Ireland archaeo-logical investigations are mainly carried out by three organisations: the Department of the Environment for Northern Ireland's Environment and Heritage Service, the Department of Archaeology and Ethnography at the Ulster Museum, and the Department of Archaeology and Palaeoecology in the School of Geosciences at the Queen's University of Belfast.

The Built Heritage staff of the Environment and Heritage Service identify, protect, record, investigate and present the ancient sites, monuments and buildings of Northern Ireland. Their work is not restoration, but preservation and conservation – seeing that our ancient monuments are protected and maintained in good repair. All known archaeological sites are registered at their headquarters in Belfast in the Sites and Monuments Record. The file on any site in Northern Ireland can be consulted. Almost 10% of all known archaeological sites are protected by 'scheduling' under the Historic

Monuments and Archaeological Objects (NI) Order 1995. The monuments registered on the schedule are selected on the basis of a number of factors including period, type, rarity, condition and locality. The work of scheduling is ongoing and, once a monument is sched-uled, the owner must obtain 'Scheduled Monument Consent' from the Department to carry out any work which would damage or disturb a monument. A further 181 sites are in 'State Care' under the same Order. These monuments are owned or leased by DOE NI or have been placed in the Department's care by their owners. The majority of the sites in this book fall into this cate-gory. The Environment and Heritage Service is also responsible for issuing licences for archaeological excava-tions in Northern Ireland. This ensures that excavations are carried out by trained, experienced and responsible individuals.

The Department of Archaeology and Ethnography at the Ulster Museum has responsibility for all archaeological

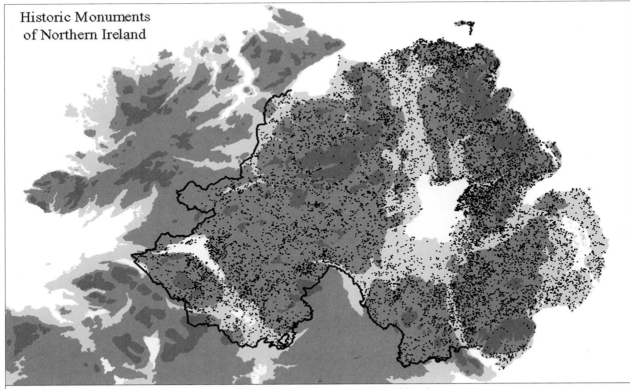

Historic Monuments of Northern Ireland

Fig. 4 Computer-generated distribution map of Historic Monuments in Northern Ireland (Michael Avery).

matters and materials in that institution. The museum collects, documents and conserves archaeological material, and the discovery of any archaeological object should, by law, always be reported to the Director. The museum presents finds from excavations in displays and is well known for its high quality exhibitions.

The Department of Archaeology and Palaeoecology in the Queen's University of Belfast School of Geosciences teaches both subjects to undergraduate students, and postgraduates and salaried staff carry out research projects on a wide variety of topics, currently including dendrochronology, radiocarbon dating, pollen analysis, osteoarchaeology, the use of computers in archaeology, aerial photography, the Giant's Ring archaeological landscape, Irish tower-houses and castles, the Neolithic settlement at Ballygalley, and the Late Bronze Age hillfort of Haughey's Fort near Armagh.

But why should tax-payers' money be used to pay for the protection of historic monuments and for their study when there are so many other worthy causes crying out for government finance? Archaeologists believe that what they do is of value to society in a number of ways. First, our historic monuments provide a link with our past, and interest in the past is a reflection of a basic human desire to understand and explore our own personal ancestry. The blossoming of local history societies in Ireland in the last two decades indicates that people do value their heritage and want to learn more about it, and local studies publications flourish. In a recent edition of *Archaeology Ireland* 176 such societies are listed in Ireland, and 67 of these are in Ulster. Second, for people living in an area a local ancient monument can become a focus, a source of pride, and reinforce a sense of past for the community. Third, our ancient and historic monuments form a rich resource for education. Visits to megalithic tombs, earthwork forts, medieval castles and abbeys can complement classroom history and open children's eyes to the past. Archaeology can provide an understanding of the economic, social and religious framework in which our ancestors lived. Ignorance is the principal agent of destruction, but if young people are encouraged to take an interest in their local heritage then that interest will stay for life and they will respect the historic landscape. The past is not a renewable resource. Once a megalithic tomb or rath has been destroyed it is gone for ever and the landscape has been robbed of a part of its past. Finally, visits to ancient monuments, heritage centres and museums are a major component of the tourist industry, helping to bring money into local communities through the sale of souvenirs, refreshments and accommodation.

While the majority of sites come under threat from ignorance there is also a deliberate threat to our heritage, one posed by the actions of 'treasure-hunters'. This 'hobby' stands largely outside the law, for the Historic Monuments and Archaeological Objects (NI) Order 1995 states that it is a criminal offence to damage or interfere with some historic monuments in any way, while it is also an offence to search for archaeological objects (with or without a metal detector) without a licence issued by the DOE NI. No archaeologist excavates for personal gain or fortune. They publish the results of their work and present any valuables that they may find to a museum, informing the public of their discoveries through the media, lectures, museum displays and books. While sterling work has been achieved by metal detectorists working in unison with archaeologists, treasure-hunters engaged in the plunder of an archaeological site plough through occupation layers and discard 'worthless' items like pottery and bone to get to what they consider are valuables. Their illegal gains are added to private collections or sold to rich buyers in foreign countries. In the USA the treasure-hunters are called 'thieves of time' and that is exactly what they are: they rob us of our shared heritage for their own individual gain.

Thirty-two monuments, most of them in the care of DOE NI Environment and Heritage Service, have been selected for study in this book. These monuments are easily accessible to the traveller and in a good state of preservation. For monuments which are not in State Care permission to visit should always be sought from the landowner. The monuments span the centuries of human occupation in the north of Ireland from prehistoric times to the industrialisation of the 19th century. The monuments are grouped together chronologically, oldest first, with each group of monuments forming a chapter. A number of the sites have multi-period use but it was decided to highlight the major period of occupation visible to the visitor as the criterion for including a site in

a particular chapter. For each site a map grid reference and a brief note on location have been included. Visitors are told what they will see when they get to the monument and the various features are then explained in more detail. Recent research on the use, function and history of the monument or similar monuments is outlined, then an attempt is made to identify any elements of continuity and change at the site. At the close of each discussion information is given on monuments of similar type to be found elsewhere in Northern Ireland. A short reading list accompanies each account to provide the reader with a list of publications which can be consulted for further information. A reading list at the end of the book gives a general introduction to archaeological study in a variety of accessible and informative publications. 'Features' accompany each chapter. These are included to provide background information on the monuments and the people who built them and also basic information on aspects of archaeological research techniques and dating methods. Most State Care monuments are open at all times but a few with caretakers have limited opening hours or may be closed because of conservation work in progress. To be sure of access, or to arrange for group admissions, please contact DOE NI Environment and Heritage Service at 5-33 Hill Street, Belfast BT1 2LA (Telephone 01232 235000).

Fowler, P J, 'Archaeology, the public and the sense of the past', *Our past before us: why do we save it?* (London, 1981), ed Lowenthal, D, and Binney, M, 56-69; Brannon, N F, *Treasure-hunting, archaeology and the law* (Belfast, 1987); Darvill, T, *Ancient monuments in the countryside*, English Heritage Archaeological Report No 5 (London, 1987); O'Connor, P J, *Living in a coded land* (Newcastle West, 1992); Bradley, R, *Altering the earth* (Edinburgh, 1993); Hunter, J, and Ralston, I, (ed) *Archaeological resource management in the UK: an introduction* (Stroud, 1993); 'Archaeology in Ireland: organisations, consultancies and courses', *Archaeology Ireland* 10.1 (1996), 37-44.

FEATURE 1   THE NATURE OF ARCHAEOLOGY

Traditional 'history' is based on the study of information contained in written sources, yet the entire story of human existence on Earth is at least 3 million years old. For 99.9% of this period of time there are no written sources to tell us about our ancestors. Indeed, the earliest written records only began around 3000 BC in Western Asia, while in other parts of the world documentation began at considerably later times. For example, document-based history is first encountered in Australia in AD 1788 after the arrival of the Old World colonists. Although some texts may be retrospective in content (for example, the earliest Irish annals), conventional history is restricted to the point in time when a society began to use the written word. In addition, we rely on the survival of written texts and our ability to decipher the script in which they were written. Faced with such limitations we must look to other sources of information to increase our knowledge of the past, and some of these can be supplied through archaeology.

Archaeology involves the retrieval and study of all forms of evidence left by our ancestors, usually by means of landscape survey and scientific excavation. In a way similar to the work of a police forensic investigation, the archaeologist assembles the clues from the surviving evidence, attempts to decipher them, and carefully constructs them as a coherent 'story'. This information is then used to support ideas or to create new theories as to how a particular culture, society or civilisa-tion lived and died. Every scrap of evidence contributes to this process, rubbish as well as treasure, from pottery, bones and wooden objects to buildings, earthworks and tombs. The archaeologist is also much concerned with climates and envi-ronments of the past and how they affected human existence (see *Feature 5: Pollen Analysis*, and *Feature 7: Dendrochronology*).

There are a number of areas in which archaeologists are interested. What technology was available to people living in the past? What types of tools did they use and for what purpose? How did they make their tools and from what materials? On what was their economy based? What was their diet? Where did they live? How did they construct their homes and what materials did they use? How did they organise their settlements? What evidence do we have for their social and ritual activ-ities? How did they organise their society? What did they do with their rubbish? How did they dispose of their dead?

While traditional history mostly reflects on the actions of the great and the powerful, whether Julius Caesar's account of his conquest of Gaul or Margaret Thatcher's memoirs of her time spent at No 10 Downing Street, archaeology is more concerned with the everyday lives of our (usually anonymous) ancestors. In this way it has much in common with social and economic history. Archaeologists attempt to make use of every source of evidence available to them when undertaking research.

They do not discard written evidence as if it were outside the boundaries of their discipline and reserved by history. Texts will be consulted if available, and in some cases the archaeologist will even challenge history. A distinction must be made, however, between prehis-toric archaeology, where written sources are not available to the researcher (for example, the mega-lithic tombs discussed in Chapter 3), and historical archaeology, where written sources are available to complement the story being told (like the Plantation sites encountered in Chapter 10). The techniques and methods used by archaeologists in the excavation of a prehistoric site are, however, broadly the same as those used at an historic site.

There can be limitations for the prehistorian when it comes to the interpretation of evidence from excavation, especially when some-thing is encountered which defies understanding. Prehistorians may have to offer some theory to explain what they have found, but they cannot force their evidence and therefore sometimes have to acknowledge doubts in their inter-pretation. One of the ways in which they can try to circumvent this problem is to look to modern 'prim-itive' societies for ethnographic parallels. For example, by studying the economic activities, culture, rituals and social organisation of modern hunter-gatherers such as the !kung bushpeople of Botswana the archaeologist may gain an insight into the way of life of the Mesolithic hunter-gatherers at

Mount Sandel and how they built their homes (see Chapter 2).

Archaeology does have weaknesses. It is particularly hindered by the problem of incomplete retrieval of evidence. An excavation usually only involves the investigation of a part of a site, since time and resources are often limited. It is only when a site is going to be totally destroyed that a total 'rescue' excavation may occur. In addition, since to excavate is to destroy, archaeologists are conscious of the fact that, where possible, areas of a site should remain untouched so that future generations of archaeologists can carry out their own investigations, perhaps with more highly developed technologies and methods of retrieval at their disposal. There is also the problem of incomplete survival of evidence. Not every object, material or structure will survive beneath the soil. Structures may have been deliberately destroyed in antiquity, while acidic soil conditions will destroy organic materials like wood, leather or clothing.

Although archaeology is considered by many people to be the study of all things ancient, in truth there are no real constraints on the time periods which can be investigated by archaeological techniques, and archaeology is the study of all aspects of the story of human existence on this planet. A 'Garbage Project' began in 1973 at Tucson,

Arizona, in the USA by examining the contents of dustbins and then moved on in 1987 to examine the

Fig. 5 Demise of a court tomb I.

Fig. 6 Demise of a court tomb II.

Fig. 7 Demise of a court tomb III.

contents of landfill rubbish dumps. As the excavator wrote, 'All archaeologists study garbage; my refuse is just fresher than most'. Among its

conclusions, the project identified that we are discarding tremendous amounts of valuable resources on a daily basis. The archaeologists identified great waste of raw materials and they argued for much greater emphasis to be placed on recyling by our society. They argued that they could identify similarities with events which had happened in another great American civilisation. The Classic period in the ancient Maya civilisation (from around AD 292 to 900) was noted for its terrible waste of materials, and it was followed by a period of decline when resources were in short supply. The Mayan solution to this shortage was to recycle. Unfortunately, they were too late and they never recovered from decline. This example emphasises that archaeology can provide lessons for our own society. It can highlight periods of disaster in the past, attempt to identify the reasons for that disaster and indicate how we can avoid repeating the same mistakes again.

Rahtz, P, *Invitation to archaeology* (Oxford, 1985); Hamlin, A, and Lynn, C J, *Pieces of the past* (HMSO, Belfast, 1988); Rathje, W L, 'Once and future landfills', *National Geographic* 179.5 (1991), 116-34. Paul Bahn's *Bluff your way in archaeology* (1989) provides a very humorous, but frighteningly accurate, overview of the discipline.

Fig. 8 The Antrim seashore (Infra-red photograph by Tony Corey).

Chapter 2

The First Settlers

1. MOUNT SANDEL Co Londonderry   C 854307

2 km S of Coleraine, signposted on the A26 to Ballymoney and reached along a signposted path beside the River Bann or through the recent housing estate.

The earliest known human occupation of Ireland dates from the Mesolithic or Middle Stone Age (8000–4000 BC). These people, who must have travelled to Ireland from Britain or continental Europe by boat or raft, followed a pre-farming economy and relied on food gathered from nature for their survival so they are sometimes called 'hunter-gatherers'. In small groups they moved into Ireland, dispersing through the country. They did not build stone monuments to their dead, as the later farming people of the Neolithic would do, and their existence is usually only identified by the finding of the flint tools they left behind them.

A window into the vanished world of the hunter-gatherers was provided in 1973 by an expansion of Coleraine's suburbs in the townland of Mount Sandel on the east bank of the River Bann. For decades Mesolithic flint artifacts had been collected from the ploughed fields in the area, so in advance of a housing development Peter Woodman organised an excavation in a field to the north-east of Mountsandel Fort. The results of this work were of great archaeological importance. In a hollow, protected from the ravages of the ploughshare, the remains of a settlement were discovered - the earliest settlement yet found in Ireland - dated by radiocarbon (see *Feature 2*) to 7000–6500 BC.

Fig. 9 Excavation of Mesolithic settlement at Mount Sandel, Co Londonderry.

On this ridge overlooking the River Bann the hunter-gatherers had built and rebuilt their circular huts. The huts had a wicker frame and a central hearth and though the roofing material is not known, sods of earth, animal skins or reeds may have been used. In and around the huts were found thousands of pieces of flint, mostly waste material left over from toolmaking, but flint tools were also found. Small pieces of worked flint (microliths) may have been used as the barbs of harpoons and there were also axes for use in heavy work. A number of large pits on the site may have been used for storing food supplies.

Fig.10 Reconstruction of Mesolithic hut at the Ulster History Park, Omagh, Co Tyrone (Ulster History Park).

The soil in the locality was acidic, but luckily large quantities of bone and hazelnut shells had been burnt before being discarded. These burnt food remains survived in the acid soil, allowing the archaeologists to suggest the diet of the Mesolithic people. Of the 2,192 bone fragments recovered, 81% were of fish such as salmon and trout, caught in the spring and summer. In the autumn, nuts, berries, fruit and eels were eaten, while in the winter stores of nutritious hazelnuts were consumed, with hunting providing the meat of wild pigs.

Distinctively Mesolithic flints have been found on the slopes down to the Bann, below the settlement, and also at Castleroe on the opposite bank of the river and in Coleraine town centre. Clearly the river, together with the resources of the sea and countryside inland, offered a livelihood for the hunter-gatherers, for much if not all of the year, over 8,000 years ago.

The Bann valley has been important throughout prehistoric and historic times. Prehistoric metalwork has been dredged from the river, a major ford provided a crossing point south of Mount Sandel in the Early Christian period, and there was an early monastery nearby at Camus. The great earthwork called Mountsandel Fort just south-west of the Mesolithic site is not firmly dated but it dominates the river and may have been of strategic importance both in the late 12th century and in the 17th century. The housing which has advanced southwards and now adjoins the Mesolithic site is the latest expression of human activity at this riverside location.

Collins, A E P, 'Excavations at Mount Sandel, lower site', *Ulster J Archaeol* 46 (1983), 1-22; Woodman, P C, *Excavations at Mount Sandel 1973-77* (HMSO, Belfast, 1985), Northern Ireland Archaeological Monographs: No 2.

FEATURE 2 | RADIOCARBON DATING

Fig.11 Furnace combustion of a pre-treated radiocarbon sample in a stream of oxygen at the Radiocarbon Laboratory, Queen's University of Belfast (Gerry McCormac).

Archaeologists work to increase our knowledge of the past, and one of the main ways they do this is by excavating. As archaeologists dig down into the soil they cut through layer after layer of deposits. Each layer is older than the one above and the layers contain archaeological features (like pits, post-holes, hearths, and house foundations) with associated artefacts. The features and finds encountered in the stratigraphy of any site allow the archaeologist to make general estimates of the date of each level of occupation, and this is

called relative dating. It was the only dating method available before the scientific revolution in dating techniques that occurred about 50 years ago. Two of these techniques, dendrochronology (see *Feature 7*) and radiocarbon dating, have been of enormous importance to archaeologists, since they make possible absolute dating of features and artefacts identified in the layers of an excavated site.

Radiocarbon dating was developed by the American scientist Willard

Libby in the 1940s. Carbon is an element that exists in three isotopic forms, two of them stable (Carbon-12 and Carbon-13), but the third (Carbon-14) radioactive and unstable. Carbon-14 is found mixed with Carbon-12 in an almost fixed ratio in the tissues of all living organisms. It is continuously being produced in the upper atmosphere by the nuclear reaction of nitrogen with cosmic radiation. The Carbon-14 combines with oxygen to form carbon dioxide which is incorporated into living tissue by photosyn-

Fig.12 The Radiocarbon Laboratory at Queen's has four high-precision liquid scintillation counters for radiocarbon dating (Gerry McCormac).

thesis. Gradually through time the Carbon-14 is broken down by radioactive decay to form nitrogen again. After the death of an organism no further Carbon-14 is taken into its tissues, the Carbon-14 that is already present begins to diminish, and the ratio of Carbon-14 to Carbon-12 begins to decrease. The rate at which any radioactive isotope decays is governed by its half-life; in the case of Carbon-14, half of any amount decays radioactively in 5,730 years. By measuring the remaining proportions of Carbon-14 to Carbon-12 atoms in an ancient sample scientists can determine the period of time that has elapsed since an organism died.

There are, however, a number of complications that have had to be addressed to make the process as accurate as possible as a dating method. Radioactive decay is a random statistical process and there will always be some error associated with the measurement of the remaining proportion of Carbon-14. This error can be expressed as a statistical probability called a 'standard deviation'. For example, a date of 3,500 radiocarbon years must be accompanied by a standard deviation to show its likely range, expressed as a plus/minus figure with the main date. To one standard deviation the date will now read as 3,500 plus/minus 100 years,

meaning that there is a 68% probability that the date for the organic material lies between the years 3600 and 3400 before present (BP). To two standard deviations there is an increased probability that the date is within the error range. The date will now read as 3500 plus/minus 200 years, meaning that there is a 95% probability that the date for the sample lies somewhere between the years 3700 and 3300 BP. Since the 'present' advances each year radiocarbon scientists have agreed on AD 1950 as the 'present' and every radiocarbon date is measured back from that year, with dates quoted as 'years BP' or 'Before Present'.

A second factor affects radiocarbon dating. The concentration of Carbon-14 in the atmosphere has varied through time and this means that radiocarbon years are not equivalent to calendar years and that they can vary with time. Radiocarbon dates, therefore, have to be checked against some other standard of known age to determine their accuracy, a process called calibration. In Northern Ireland Mike Baillie's oak tree-ring calendar (see *Feature 7*) was used to calibrate radiocarbon dates in the Palaeoecology Centre at the Queen's University of Belfast. Blocks of 20 growth rings of known tree-ring calendar date were sampled and submitted for radiocarbon dating from every point in time for the last 7,000 years. A calibration curve was created by plotting the calendar dates of annual oak growth rings against the radiocarbon dates of the same rings. This work was undertaken by Gordon Pearson who produced a high-precision calibration curve incorporating radiocarbon dates which had probable errors of only plus/minus 20 years. The Queen's University Radiocarbon Laboratory is renowned throughout the archaeological world for its important work. Recent research, under Gerry McCormac, has resulted in a revised chronology for the famous Stonehenge monument in Wiltshire, and the development of a radiocarbon calibration curve for the southern hemisphere using New Zealand kaikawaka trees.

Aitken, M J, *Science-based dating in archaeology* (Harlow, 1990), 56-119; Bowman, S, *Radiocarbon dating* (London, 1990); Baillie, M G L, 'Dating the past', *The illustrated archaeology of Ireland* (Dublin, 1991), ed Ryan, M, 15-19; Lanting, J and Brindley, A, 'Radiocarbon dating', *Archaeology Ireland* 5.1 (1991), 24-6; Renfrew, C, and Bahn, P, *Archaeology: theories, methods and practice* (London, 1991), 121-29; Cleal, R H J, Walker, K E, and Montague, R, *Stonehenge in its landscape: 20th-century excavations*, English Heritage Archaeological Report No 10 (London, 1995).

Fig.13 The Giant's Ring, Co Down (Infra-red photograph by Tony Corey).

Chapter 3

The Pioneering Farmers

4 km NE of Carrickmore. From the minor road which runs NW from the B4 between Pomeroy and Sixmilecross a path leads round the S shore of Lough Mallon to the monument.

The tomb is set on an exposed glacial hill at the west side of Lough Mallon. It commands extensive views of the surrounding countryside, much of which is shrouded in blanket bog. The visitor will see an elegant stone cairn, trapezoidal in plan, decreasing in width and height from a wide south-east front. The long sides of the cairn are revetted with drystone walls. There is a semicircular 'court' at the front of the tomb, its curving facade constructed of widely-spaced stone uprights with dry-stone walling set between each upright. In the centre of this facade is the entrance to a burial gallery, its doorway framed by two jamb stones surmounted by a massive lintel (the highest point of the tomb). The burial gallery is divided into three chambers by pairs of jamb stones. The gallery with its chambers was originally roofed with flat slabs and covered by the cairn.

The site was excavated from 1979 to 1982 by Claire Foley because the monument was threatened by a land reclamation scheme. Before the excavation no one had imagined that an entire court tomb was hidden beneath the peat. Only a few large stones protruded above the ground surface, one of which turned out to be the lintel. The visitor will see moss growing on the top of the lintel and this marks the level to which the stone was once buried. The archaeologists began by removing the peat and heather, then they had to remove tons of loose and collapsed cairn stones to reveal the original outline of the tomb. When this initial work was completed it became clear that this was an unexpectedly well-preserved court tomb. The peat had protected the monument for centuries and the archaeologists now had a chance to study and record a fine example of Neolithic architecture.

The amount of collapsed stone removed from the monument suggests that its covering cairn originally stood some 2 to 3 m in height. The burial gallery was roofed with overlapping (corbelled) stone slabs. This roof and much cairn material had collapsed into the burial chamber after the tomb had been abandoned, but the lower courses of large corbelled granite blocks were still in position. Thin sandstone slabs found lying in the burial gallery may have been used to bridge the gap between the granite corbels.

Court tombs derive their name from their most prominent feature, the court at the front of the tomb, but in the past they have also been called 'court cairns' and 'horned cairns'. The court area was probably used for ritual or ceremonial activity. At Creggandevesky cremated human

Fig.14 Court tomb at Creggandevesky, Co Tyrone, following excavation and conservation.

The grave-goods that accompanied the dead included flint arrowheads, scrapers, knives, a javelin head, an awl and a necklace of 112 stone beads. The fragmentary remains of seven Neolithic pots were also found. These objects may have been intended for use in an afterlife; they may have been the prized possessions in life of the people who were buried in the tomb.

Almost 400 court tombs are known in Ireland, and new sites are still being discovered. For instance, a massive tomb was found during fieldwork at Antynanum, Co Antrim, in 1991. The vast majority of the tombs are in the northern half of the island, with notable concentrations in Co Sligo, Co Mayo, mid Tyrone, south Down, south Armagh and north Antrim. In Tyrone there are eleven court tombs within a 10-mile radius of Creggandevesky. Similar tombs are found in Scotland, the Isle of Man and on both sides of the Severn estuary in Britain, but there is still debate over where this type of tomb originated.

bone was found in several areas of the tomb, especially at the entrance and in front of the burial gallery. While cremation appears to have been the common form of burial in court tombs, inhumations have been found at a number of sites. There may have been inhumations at Creggandevesky but acidic soil conditions have destroyed all traces. No cremated bone, but numerous grave-goods were found in the second chamber so perhaps a now-vanished inhumation was placed in this part of the tomb. In all, the remains of five males, seven females, one adolescent and eight other individuals were identified. The cremated bone provided samples for radiocarbon dating (see *Feature 2*) which indicates that the tomb was in use around 3500 BC.

Creggandevesky was built by a community of early farmers. Pollen evidence (see *Feature 5*) indicates that hazel trees grew in the area after the collapse of the tomb, but the excavation showed that there was some Bronze Age activity at the narrow end of the cairn and it seems that the site was not forgotten. As the bog began to grow, however, the surrounding land became unproductive and the farmers abandoned the area (see also Chapter 4: Beaghmore Stone Circles and Drumskinny Stone Circle). The bog eventually swallowed up the court tomb until modern farming activity led to its rediscovery. The owner was so impressed with the monument as the excavation progressed that he agreed not to remove it, and it was subsequently taken into State Care. Creggandevesky tomb is a fitting memorial to the engineering skills and afterlife beliefs of our farming ancestors who worked this land 5,500 years ago.

Other court tombs include Audleystown, Co Down (J 562504), Cregganconroe, Co Tyrone (H 663758), Dooey's Cairn (D 021182) and Ossian's Grave (D 213284), both in Co Antrim, and Aghanaglack Dual Court Tomb in Co Fermanagh (H 098436).

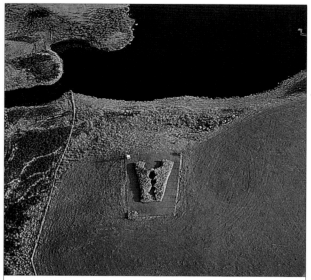

Fig.15 Aerial view of the court tomb at Creggandevesky.

Foley, C, *Pieces of the past* (HMSO, Belfast, 1988), ed Hamlin, A, and Lynn, C J, 3-5; O'Kelly, M J, *Early Ireland: an introduction to Irish prehistory* (Cambridge, 1989), 85-92; Mallory, J P, and McNeill, T E, *The archaeology of Ulster* (Belfast, 1991), 56-63.

3. LEGANANNY DOLMEN   Portal tomb   Co Down   J 288434

6.4 km S of Dromara and 8 km NW of Castlewellan.

Legananny Dolmen stands at the side of a narrow lane on the southern fringes of Slieve Croob, near the source of the River Lagan, and from beside it the visitor can enjoy a magnificent view of the Mourne Mountains in the distance. The stone skeleton of a Neolithic burial monument, Legananny is an impressive example of a 'tripod' portal tomb.

The large capstone is perched on three upright stones, and the two tall pillars at the front are called 'portal stones' as they framed the entrance to the burial chamber. The coffin-shaped capstone slopes down from the portal stones and rests on the third pillar, the backstone. Slight traces of the stone cairn which originally covered the tomb can be seen on all sides except the east, where the farm lane runs by. At most portal tombs the cairns are poorly preserved, but where evidence does survive, as at Ballykeel, Co Armagh, they tend to be similar to the long cairns found with court tombs. A stone slab lying inside the chamber may belong to the cairn or it may be part of the burial chamber. At some portal tombs stone slabs were set against the portals and backstones to serve as sides to the burial chamber, but at Legananny these stones are absent. Perhaps this tomb had side walls of wood or dry-stone which have decayed or collapsed.

Fig.16 Legananny Dolmen, Co Down, with the Mourne Mountains in the distance.

Though there are reports of 'urns' having been found in the past, Legananny has never been excavated. The results of excavations at other portal tombs in Northern Ireland have generally been disappointing since acidic soil conditions in the burial chambers have destroyed the bone

remains. To get some idea of the Neolithic people buried in a portal tomb we have to look south, to Poulnabrone in the limestone Burren of Co Clare, where Ann Lynch excavated in 1986. Here the well preserved burial chamber was found to contain the remains of between 16 and 22 adults and six children, including a baby. All the adults except one had died before the age of 30. The bones had been placed in the chamber in a disarticulated state, and this may mean that the dead had been buried elsewhere and moved, or left exposed to decay before the remains were taken to their final resting-place (see also this chapter: The Giant's Ring). The dead were provided with a variety of grave-goods, including bone pins, a polished stone axe, a bone pendant, flint and chert scrapers and coarse pottery.

There are 174 known portal tombs in Ireland, the majority of them located in the northern half of the country, showing a similar distribution to court tombs (see this chapter: Creggandevesky). Thirty-five are found in south-east Ireland, and similar tombs occur in Wales and Cornwall. The time at which portal tombs were in use during the long Neolithic period has not yet been established, but there are similarities between court and portal tombs and there may be a connection between the two classes. Portal tombs may have evolved from court tombs, or the two types may have been in use at the same time. Only further archaeological research can establish the chronological and evolutionary relationship between portal and court tombs.

Fig.17 Legananny Dolmen at the beginning of the 20th century, Welch Collection, RW 1908 (Ulster Museum).

The imposing outline of portal tombs, especially when cleared of their covering cairns, have made them striking features of the landscape and a focus of attention and curiosity for 4,000 years or more. In local tradition they are seen as 'Druid's Altars' or 'Diarmuid and Grainne's Beds', or even the work of 'giants'. In recent times they have been favoured above all other prehistoric monuments by the producers of post-cards and calendars, and Legan_anny Dolmen has appeared on the cover of many books and leaflets. It may be the most frequently illustrated example of its type in the whole of Ireland, and it is depicted on a large mural by the artist William Conor called 'Ulster Past and Present' in the Ulster Museum. It is still very much part of our cultural heritage after four millennia.

Other portal tombs include Ballykeel, Co Armagh (H 995213), Ballyrenan, Co Tyrone (H 373832), Goward and Kilfeaghan, Co Down (J 244310 and J 232154), and Ticloy, Co Antrim (D 232118).

Collins, A E P, 'Ballykeel dolmen and cairn, Co Armagh', *Ulster J Archaeol* 28 (1965), 47-70; Ó Nualláin, S, 'Irish portal graves: topography, siting and distribution', *JRSAI* 113 (1983), 75-105; Lynch, A, 'Poulnabrone - a stone in time', *Archaeology Ireland 2.3* (1988), 105-7.

4. KNOCKMANY	Passage tomb Co Tyrone	H 547559

2.8 km NW of Augher, on a hill in Knockmany Forest Park, reached by a winding uphill path through the forest from the car-park on the NW side of the hill.

On a hilltop commanding superb views south over the Clogher valley is an earthern mound with a modern roof-light set on its summit. On the south side of the mound a small flight of concrete steps leads down to the entrance to a chamber, its walls built of concrete blocks, rendered and painted white. Clearly this chamber is modern, but within are the remains of a prehistoric tomb - a passage tomb - built of large slabs of local sandstone set on end. The visitor will see elaborate designs pecked into the surface of several of the wall slabs. These geometric motifs - circles, zig-zags, lozenges and triangles - are among the best examples of prehistoric art known in Northern Ireland.

Until 1959 the decorated stones of the tomb lay open to the elements, but weathering and vandalism were gradually destroying the decoration on the surface of the slabs. To prevent any further deterioration the then Ministry of Finance decided that the monument should be covered with a roofed structure, but before this was done the site was excavated by Pat Collins. His work showed that the ancient burial chamber stood in a circular cairn of boulders which may originally have covered the entire monument. Surrounding and probably covering the cairn was a thick deposit of earth, its outer edge kept in place by a rough kerb of smaller stones. All trace of the tomb roof was gone but it is likely that it was covered with similar slabs to those used in the walls. No evidence was found for an approach passage into the chamber, the feature which gives this class of tomb its name. Only a few scraps of cremated bone were found in the chamber, and no grave-goods were retrieved.

Harold Meek, Ancient Monuments architect at the time, was given the task of building an appropriate 'house' to enclose the monument, and a rectangular chamber of concrete blocks was constructed, surmounted by a flat roof with a roof-light. The work was based on comparable reinforced concrete coverings built by the Ministry of Works in Scotland at Cairnpapple, West Lothian, and at the Knowe of Unstan, Stenness, in the Orkney Islands. An earthen skin was added to simulate the appearance of a mound. The tomb lacked an entrance passage in antiquity but some form of entrance was needed to allow visitors to see the inside of the tomb and the decorated stones, so a modern entrance with concrete steps was created on the south side of the newly piled-up mound.

The passage tomb is a third type of megalithic tomb dating from the Neolithic period. Passage tombs are named from the passage which usually leads to the burial chamber. This passage is thought to have provided access so that the tomb could be used over several generations before its final sealing. The absence of a passage at Knockmany suggests that the tomb may have been built, used and sealed as a single episode. The Knockmany chamber is roughly rectangular in shape, but circular, polygonal and cruciform plans are also found. Some 229

Fig.18 Knockmany passage tomb, Co Tyrone, at the beginning of the 20th century, Welch Collection, RW 1910 (Ulster Museum).

passage tombs are known in Ireland, the most famous of which is Newgrange, Co Meath, but they are also found in western Wales, Scotland, Spain, Brittany and southern

Fig. 19 Lifting the passage tomb's fallen stone slabs during conservation in 1961.

Scandinavia. In Ireland these tombs are sometimes grouped in great cemeteries, as at Carrowmore, Co Sligo or in the Boyne Valley, Co Meath. In Ulster there are groups in north Antrim and in the Clogher valley, but many passage tombs are isolated monuments in the land-scape. Recent research suggests that the earliest and simplest passage tombs in Ireland are those in north Antrim and Co Sligo. The later tombs, like those in the Boyne Valley, are of greater size and are very much more elaborate.

The motifs used by the Neolithic people to decorate the Knockmany slabs cannot be interpreted with any certainty. We can only guess what they may have meant: magic spells, perhaps, or messages to deities, names of the dead, a record of tribes or events, or simply art for art's sake? The art at Knockmany is similar to art found in passage tombs at Newgrange, Knowth, Loughcrew and Fourknocks, all in Co Meath. Dates from these larger sites suggest the period of 3000 to 2500 BC for the building of passage tombs like Knockmany.

In its forest clearing on a hilltop, Knockmany cairn is visible from far away, and in the past it must always have been an important feature of the landscape. It is not surprising, therefore, that stories grew up round the monument. By the 12th century it was believed that the hill – *Cnoc mBáine* – was the burial place of Queen Báine, wife of Tuathal Teachtmhar, who is mentioned in the *Annals of the Four Masters* under the year AD 111. Locally, the tomb is called Annia's Cove and tradition names it as the home of a hag called Áine or Annia. In the 18th century the writer William Carleton, who lived close by and often visited the tomb, saw the hill as the home of 'Finn McCoul and his wife Oonagh', while graffiti on the stones suggest that the monument was a favourite picnic site in the 19th century. The tomb has been a focus of attention and wonder for more than 4,000 years.

Other passage tombs include Slieve Gullion South Cairn, Co Armagh (J 025203) and Magheraboy, Co Antrim (D 035437).

Collins, A E P, and Meek, H A, 'Knockmany chambered cairn, Co Tyrone', *Ulster J Archaeol* 23 (1960), 2-8; Sheridan, A, 'Megaliths and megalomania: an account and interpretation of the development of passage tombs in Ireland', *Journal of Irish Archaeology* 3 (1985-6), 17-30; Eogan, G, *Knowth and the passage tombs of Ireland* (London, 1986); Mallory, J P, and McNeill, T E, *The archaeology of Ulster* (Belfast, 1991), 65-9; O'Sullivan, M, and Scarry, J, *Megalithic art in Ireland* (Dublin, 1993).

Footnote: The entrance to the tomb chamber is locked. Visitors wishing to enter the chamber should make prior arrangements with the DOE NI Environment and Heritage Service (see p 5).

Fig. 20 Knockmany: geometric motifs on wall slab in chamber.

5. THE GIANT'S RING | Henge monument and passage tomb   Co Down   J 327677

In the outskirts of Belfast, 6.5 km from the city centre and 1.2 km S of Shaw's Bridge, off the Ballylesson road in the townland of Ballynahatty. Well signposted with a large car-park at the entrance.

Though it is close to Belfast, the Giant's Ring lies in open countryside, on a distinct plateau in a bend in the River Lagan. For the people of the city it has long been a favourite destination for a Sunday afternoon stroll or a summer picnic, but how many of its visitors realise how important this landscape was 4,000 years ago, and still is for archaeological research today?

The Giant's Ring is a huge circular enclosure, 180 m in diameter. The massive surrounding bank is 4 m high and

18 m wide, and the enclosed area is about 2.8 hectares. From the top of the bank there are magnificent views of the Lagan valley, Belfast and the hills beyond. Near the middle of the enclosure is a stone tomb, now denuded of its original covering cairn. It looks at first rather like a portal tomb, with a sloping dislodged capstone, but its plan indicates that it is probably a passage tomb (see this chapter: Knockmany).

Several excavations have been carried out at the Giant's

Fig. 21 Aerial view of the Giant's Ring, Co Down. The ritual enclosures of Ballynahatty 5 and 6 are visible as crop-marks in the foreground, while small circular crop-marks are visible at the top right (Barrie Hartwell).

Ring, in 1917, 1929 and 1954. Henry Lawlor examined the tomb in 1917 but found no evidence for its date. It is generally agreed that the tomb, the only survivor of an extensive passage tomb cemetery, is earlier than the ring, and that the earthwork enclosure was set out round it. The 1950s excavation showed that the bank was created by scraping up soil and stones from inside the area rather than by digging a well-defined ditch as might have been expected.

The Giant's Ring is the type of enclosure called by archaeologists a henge monument. It is not closely dated but a date of around 2000 BC is possible (Late Neolithic – Early Bronze Age). Its scale indicates that very substantial resources of time and effort were available to build the earthworks. Henge monuments are believed to

have been regional or tribal meeting places, used perhaps for religious ceremonies, commercial gatherings or social events, but excavation has so far thrown little light on their exact functions.

The Giant's Ring was, however, only one element in a complex prehistoric landscape. In recent years Barrie Hartwell of the Queen's University of Belfast has been studying this landscape and revealing its complexities. From the 19th century there are records of megalithic tombs, standing stones and flat cemeteries in the fields around the Giant's Ring, but most of these were long ago destroyed without any investigation. Barrie Hartwell has, through air photography, discovered a rich range of crop-mark sites in the arable fields around the monument and has carried out a series of excavations to establish the nature and date of some of these sites. To date the excavations have identified nine structures formerly unknown, the most notable of which are two Late Neolithic circular enclosures, dating from about 3000 – 2500 BC and located one inside the other. The oval, outer enclosure, over 90 m long, was delimited by a double line of massive wooden posts set in pits 2 m deep. Within this clearly demarcated area was an inner enclosure, 16 m in diameter, similarly constructed. An entrance in its circuit led through a planked façade to what may have been a mortuary platform, enclosed by four massive posts, where the dead could have been placed in security until the soft tissue had rotted or been scavenged (the process known as excarnation), the skeletal remains then being either inhumed or cremated elsewhere in the vicinity. The inner enclosure had then been ceremonially dismantled, burnt and buried, perhaps as part of a death ritual.

The impact of the Giant's Ring on the historic landscape must always have been recognised, if only because of its great size, and people not surprisingly attributed its building to a giant. The stone wall round the outer base of the bank was built in 1841 to protect the monument. An inscription facing the carpark commemorates its building by Lord Dungannon who 'earnestly recommends it [the ring] to the care of his successors'. In 1882 the Giant's Ring was one of only three northern sites in the schedule to the first Ancient Monuments Protection Act (with Navan Fort and the Mound at Downpatrick), and it has been in State Care since the early years of this century.

Barrie Hartwell's research is allowing us to glimpse an impressive continuity of use of what he calls the 'ceremonial landscape' around the Giant's Ring during the Neolithic and Bronze Ages. The range of burial monuments recorded at Ballynahatty indicates that the area was a centre for ritual for perhaps a thousand years. Burial practices changed, but people continued to come to this ceremonial area to bury their dead, as their ancestors had done before them. The recent excavations also point to the land not having been under cultivation in the Neolithic and Bronze Ages. Though the light soils are ideally suited to arable farming, it seems that the land was set aside from farming, again indicating a special status for the area. Though now farmed, the area is mainly open land with few buildings, and it is tempting to suggest that it has never ceased to be in some way 'special' in the eyes of the people of the Lagan Valley.

Collins, A E P, 'Excavations at the Giant's Ring, Ballynahatty', *Ulster J Archaeol* 20 (1957), 44–50; Hartwell, B, 'Ballynahatty – a prehistoric ceremonial centre', *Archaeology Ireland* 5.4 (1991), 12–15; Hartwell, B, 'Late Neolithic ceremonies', *Archaeology Ireland* 8.4 (1994), 10–13.

Fig. 22 The Giant's Ring: massive post-holes of inner ritual enclosure (Ballynahatty 6) revealed during excavation (Barrie Hartwell).

FEATURE 3 LIFE IN THE NEOLITHIC

The Neolithic (New Stone Age) in Ireland lasted from about 4000 to 2500 BC. In this long period there was a major change in society from the hunter-gatherer traditions of the Mesolithic to a new economy based on farming. Some of these farmers may have been descendants of the hunter-gatherer people, and some could have been new settlers arriving from Britain and Continental Europe. The appearance of new technologies for working stone, a more complex social organisation and the introduction of domesticated animals, like cattle and sheep, all tend to support the view that some degree of migration of new people into Ireland occurred at this time.

In contrast to the hunter-gatherers, the Neolithic farmers had a more settled way of life, working their plots of land and tending their stock. The production of food on the farm meant that they were not dependent on the natural resources of the countryside, although fishing, hunting and the gathering of wild plants and fruit probably supplemented their diet. Their basic farming techniques (planting and harvesting), their plants (wheat and barley) and their animals (cattle, sheep and goats) are still to be found on farms to this day, though methods and breeds have obviously changed greatly.

Our information about the people is largely based on the human remains (see *Feature 4*) recovered from their tombs (known as 'megaliths' from the large stones used in their construction). The greater certainty

Fig. 23 Excavation of a Neolithic house at Ballyharry, Co Antrim, with pipe-line in background.

of food supply and a settled pattern of life allowed communities to expend effort and resources on the construction of stone burial monuments, probably as expressions of their religious and social beliefs. While it seems that only a selection of individuals were buried in these monuments, those remains which have been examined suggest that the majority of the population were dead by the age of 30 to 35. There was a high death rate among the

very young and diseases like arthritis were common.

Excavation has uncovered Neolithic houses at a small number of sites in Northern Ireland, including Ballynagilly, Co Tyrone, and Ballyharry and Ballygalley, both in Co Antrim. Other examples have been discovered elsewhere in Ireland. These houses were built of timber and were rectangular, with pitched, thatched roofs and open hearths. The buildings could have housed a family of up to a dozen individuals. In size they were probably not unlike the thatched houses occupied in rural Ireland into the present century. Other settlement sites, perhaps camp-sites, have been found in coastal areas like the sand-dunes near Dundrum, Co Down and White Park Bay, Co Antrim. At Lyles Hill and Donegore Hill, both in south Antrim, two large enclosed hilltop settlements have been identified and partly excavated.

Fig. 24 Reconstruction of a Neolithic house at the Ulster History Park, Omagh, Co Tyrone (Ulster History Park).

Just as farmhouses today are only a part of a greater rural network of fields and roads, so too were the Neolithic farmhouses. In north Mayo extensive field systems have been found beneath peat bogs and similar field systems may exist in the peat-shrouded landscapes of Ulster, such as the uplands of Antrim and Tyrone.

Flint and sometimes other stones were used for making tools and weapons, the stone either being collected as nodules on the Antrim coast or mined from open-cast workings like the one on Ballygalley Head, Co Antrim. At Tievebulliagh, Co Antrim and Brockley on Rathlin Island, a tough rock associated with volcanic activity called porcellanite was collected for the manufacture of polished stone axes, ideal for use in forest clearance. Since this rock is very rare, it is probably true to say that any examples of porcellanite polished stone axes found outside the north-east of Ireland have been transported through trade or exchange. Contacts between different communities throughout the British Isles seem likely since porcellanite axes have been found in places as far apart as Aberdeenshire and southern England.

For most Neolithic people life may have been short and harsh, judged by our modern standards, but we must not think of them as 'primitive' or unintelligent. They lived to as high a standard as their technology allowed. They were superbly skilled in working and handling stone, for example, and probably also bone and leather. Doubtless they had the same human fears, affections and foibles as modern people. The time, effort and resources spent on building magnificent tombs suggests that these dispersed farming communities may have grouped together for building projects, unity being demonstrated in the presence of death. The reverence shown to ancestors may also have been a way of underlining rights to the farmland which they had inherited and which provided their livelihood. The tombs may contain the bones of the leaders of those distant societies.

Bradley, R, *The social foundations of prehistoric Britain* (London, 1984), 6-67; Sheridan, J A, 'Porcellanite artifacts: a new survey', *Ulster J Archaeol* 49 (1986), 19-32; Cooney, G, 'Life in the Neolithic', *Archaeology Ireland* 3.2 (1989), 51-4; Cooney, G, and Grogan, E, *Irish prehistory: a social perspective* (Dublin, 1994), 35-94; Simpson, D D A, 'The Neolithic settlement site at Ballygalley, Co Antrim', *Annus Archaeologiae: proceedings of the OIA winter conference 1993* (Dublin, 1995), ed Grogan, E, and Mount, C, 37-44; Crothers, N, 'Ballyharry's game', *Archaeology Ireland* 10.4 (1996), 12-14.

Fig. 25 Tievebulliagh, Co Antrim.

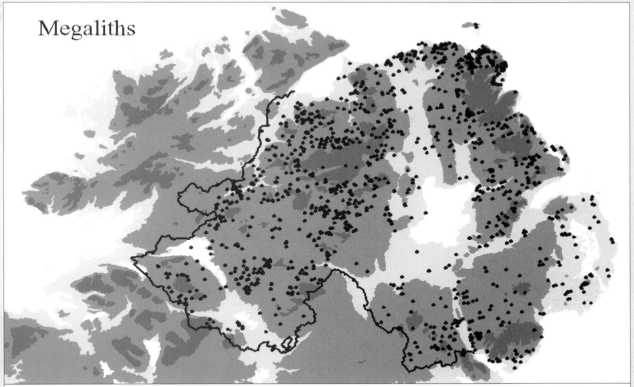

Megaliths

Fig. 26 Computer-generated distribution map of megaliths in Northern Ireland (Michael Avery).

FEATURE 4   HUMAN BONE STUDIES

Osteoarchaeology is the study of both human and animal bones (see also Feature 11) recovered during archaeological investigations. This research is very important in reconstructing the lifestyles of people in the past since it provides crucial information of demographic, economic and social significance. The work of the osteoarchaeologist requires great patience, a meticulous attention to detail, and a comprehensive knowledge of skeletal anatomy and pathology since even the smallest fragment of bone may have a story to tell.

During the course of an excavation the discovery of human skeletal remains can bring us face to face with our ancestors. When this occurs an osteoarchaeologist, if possible, is called onto the site. The remains are recorded where they have been found, before being carefully collected and transported to the laboratory where each skeleton is individually washed, labelled, and then studied. The osteoarchaeologist uses a wide variety of scientific methods on the remains, some of which are for adult skeletons, while others are designed for studying infant and juvenile skeletons. By using the methods suitable for each individual, the specialist is able to gain an overall picture of a population's age and sex profiles, average stature and general standard of health.

The bones of the pelvis are the most useful in determining the sex of a skeleton. Female pelvic bones are adapted for childbirth, being generally lower and broader than the equivalent male bones. The size and shape of the skull and long bones are also helpful indicators in identifying an individual's sex, since males tend to have large, prominent muscle attachments. It is, however, extremely difficult to tell whether a child's skeleton is male or female since there

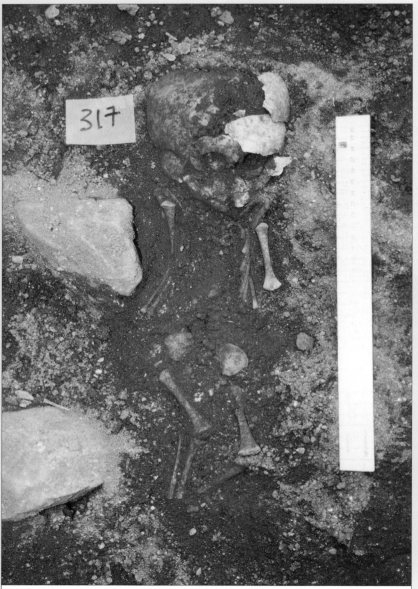

Fig. 27 Skeleton of an infant discovered during excavation at Castle Carra, Co Antrim (Eileen Murphy).

measuring the length of a skeleton's long bones and placing the figures obtained within pre-prepared mathmatical equations it is also possible to calculate a person's height at the time of death.

Not all human skeletons retrieved from archaeological contexts, however, are found in the form of carefully laid out burials; cremated skeletons are commonly encountered at some types of prehistoric burial sites. The cremated bones are generally broken and severely damaged by the heat produced on

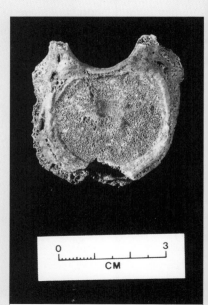

Fig. 28 Evidence of degenerative joint disease displayed in a human thoracic vertebra from Doonbought Fort, Co Antrim (Eileen Murphy).

are only very slight skeletal differences between the two sexes before the onset of puberty. Numerous methods are available for determining the age at which an individual died. Until a person is approximately 25 years of age teeth and bones are developing at a fairly uniform rate. In younger individuals it is possible to examine the stage of

development that their bones and teeth had reached and accurately determine their age at death. After the age of 25 the body starts to degenerate. These changes do not occur as uniformly as the developmental changes observed in younger individuals but it is still possible to estimate the age at death of an adult to within a ten-year period. By

the funeral pyre. Certain fragments such as teeth and pieces of skull, however, can still provide information about the age and sex of the person under study. On occasion, knowledge of the grave goods which accompanied a body onto the pyre can be gained from an examination of fragments of glass or metal which melted and fused with the bones in the extreme heat of the fire. An excavation in 1987 at Dun Ruadh, a Late Neolithic henge monument in Co Tyrone, revealed the presence of an Early Bronze Age cist burial set in the monument's bank. The burial contained the cremated bones of two individuals, an adult woman over 30 years of age, and a child approximately four years old. The burial is considered to consist of a mother and her child, both of whom had died at the same time.

Another aspect of osteoarchaeology is palaeopathology - the study of diseases which afflicted people in the past. A person may have endured a number of diseases during the course of his or her life, each of which may have left its own signature on the bones. An obvious example would be a broken limb. If the fracture healed with little or no medical care the bone may have an abnormal appearance consisting of two or more malaligned sections. A second common category of palaeopathology is degenerative joint diseases, which may be directly related to ageing processes or to occupational activities. An osteoarchaeologist can identify conditions such as osteoarthritis by looking for the presence of small boney growths (osteophytes), bone porosity and patches of polished bone (eburnation) at joint surfaces. Other diseases manifest themselves in a more subtle manner. Twenty-two skeletons were discovered during an excavation in the interior of a medieval fort at Doonbought, Co Antrim. One individual, a child aged six or seven, was found to have suffered from a very rare condition called hydrocephalus, caused by a problem in the absorption of cerebrospinal fluid in the brain and spinal cord. Although in some cases the disease can be

secondary to a primary illness, such as chronic chest infection, in this case it was thought to have been congenital. A build-up of fluid between the brain and the inner skull surface caused the skull bones to move apart, making the child's head enlarged and globular in form. It is possible that the individual's cause of death was related to hydrocephalus.

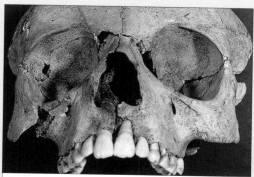

Fig. 29 Pitting (cribra orbitalia) displayed inside the eye sockets of a medieval child from Doonbought Fort, Co Antrim, indicates possible anaemia (Eileen Murphy).

The results of poor standards of dental hygene or a diet rich in sugary food can cause dental lesions. Caries, or tooth cavities, are caused by the fermentation by bacteria of sugary food substances present on teeth. Skeletal remains suggest that many of our ancestors probably suffered great pain from dental caries. In addition, dental diseases tend not to occur separately from one another. If people were suffering from caries they probably had associated abscesses and periodontal disease, also extremely painful, conditions resulting in tooth loss and perhaps even death.

Osteoarchaeologists never undertake their work lightly and they are ever conscious of the respect and dignity with which human remains must be treated. When a population of skeletons has been fully examined, and

the information about each individual accurately recorded and photographed, the bones are returned to the excavator of the site who is then responsible for their storage or reburial in a suitable resting-place.

Human bone studies have always been a very important component of archaeological investigations but the next few years will be a particularly exciting time for osteoarchaeological research. A host of new scientific methods are currently being implemented, each designed to obtain more information from skeletal remains, and these seem set to expand our understanding of life (and death) in the past. The new techniques being adopted include the extraction of DNA from bones for population and palaeopathological studies, the use of electron microscopy for studying tissue, chemical isotope analysis for dietary reconstruction, and the application of medical techniques for the study of palaeopathological lesions.

Simpson, D D A, Weir, D A, and Wilkinson, J L, 'Excavations at Dun Ruadh, Crouck, Co Tyrone', *Ulster J Archaeol* 54-55 (1991-92), 36-47; Murphy, E M, and McNeill, T E, 'Human remains excavated at Doonbought Fort, Co Antrim, 1969', *Ulster J Archaeol* 56 (1993), 120-38; Power, C, 'Reconstructing patterns of health and dietary change in Irish prehistoric populations', *Ulster J Archaeol* 56 (1993), 9-17; Chamberlain, A, *Human remains* (London, 1994); Roberts, C, and Manchester, K, *The archaeology of disease*, second edition (Stroud, 1995); Hurl, D P, and Murphy, E M, 'Life and death in a County Antrim tower house', *Archaeology Ireland* 10.2 (1996), 20-23.

Fig. 30 Beaghmore, Co Tyrone (Infra-red photograph by Tony Corey).

Chapter 4

The Age of the Bronzeworkers

4 km W of Carncastle on the minor road to Dunteige Bridge.

Dunteige wedge tomb stands on a small height overlooking a region of bleak upland terrain. The visitor sees two double lines of stone walling, aligned from south-west to north-east. Both of the inner walls are of large, upright slabs, and the area between is filled with debris, with a large stone slab lying among the rubble. At the south-west end of the tomb is a large, upright stone slab. The two lines of outer walling are of smaller upright stone slabs, best preserved along the north-west side where ten substantial boulders are visible. Dunteige is a particularly well-preserved example of a wedge tomb. It has never been excavated using modern archaeological techniques but was one of four megalithic structures investigated in 1869-70 by Lord Antrim and Dr Holden.

Wedge tombs form the largest class of Irish megalithic tombs, with some 470 known examples, distributed mainly in the southern and western parts of the island. In Ulster they are found in counties Donegal, Londonderry, Tyrone and Fermanagh with a few outliers in east Antrim, of which Dunteige is one. Wedge tombs take their name from their characteristic wedge-shaped plan and profile. An oval or rectangular cairn covered a flat stone-slab roof over a long burial gallery. At Dunteige the covering cairn has been removed, but the two outer lines of stone slabs mark its extent since these slabs were the cairn's revetting kerbstones. The slabs which roofed the gallery have been removed, except for the single slab now lying inside the gallery. Wedge tomb galleries are generally wide and high at the entrance but slope downwards and inwards to a narrow, low back. This can be seen best at sites which have been denuded of their covering cairn, as at Dunteige, although here the narrow gallery is now blocked up by cairn debris. In common with other wedge tombs a small antechamber is present at the entrance to Dunteige. At some stage in the monument's life access to the gallery was deliberately sealed by the placing of a huge stone slab across the entrance.

The date of the origin of wedge tombs is still in doubt. Only about twenty tombs have been excavated in Ireland and the archaeological material recovered has been very meagre. At Boviel, Co Londonderry, Late Neolithic pottery and tools were discovered in the tomb. At eight other sites Beaker pottery of the Early Bronze Age has been found. It is possible that wedge tombs originated in the Late Neolithic but continued to be built and reused in the Bronze Age, which began around 2500-2000 BC.

The landscape around Dunteige is rich in archaeological

Fig. 31 Dunteige Wedge Tomb, Co Antrim, in the early 20th century. Green Collection, WAG 1639 (Ulster Folk & Transport Museum).

remains, including a promontory fort, old field systems, a standing stone, abandoned settlements, a rath, a cairn and earthwork enclosures. These hilltops are now only suitable for cattle and sheep farming, not for the intensive agriculture practised on lowland farms. As a result many monuments which might be cleared or ploughed in the lowlands have survived in the uplands. Dunteige and the neighbouring townlands make up what is called an 'archaeological landscape' in which the human presence in and influence on the landscape from prehistoric to modern times is reflected in a rich variety of different monuments which survive.

Among the most recent of these monuments is a polygonal flat-topped basalt boulder near the wedge tomb with Latin crosses incised on its top and north faces. There is no tradition of a church having existed on this site and the boulder is probably a Roman Catholic mass rock used during Penal times, in the years between the 1690s and the late 18th century. While beliefs and rites may change or be abandoned over the millennia, the close proximity of the mass rock and the wedge tomb acts as a reminder of the religious activity of our ancestors expressed by the monuments they left behind in the landscape.

Other wedge tombs include Ballygroll (C 533137), Ballybriest (near a court tomb) (H 762885) and Boviel (C 730078), all in Co Londonderry, and Loughmacrory, Co Tyrone (H 586776).

O'Kelly, M J, *Early Ireland: an introduction to Irish prehistory* (Cambridge, 1989), 115–22; Mallory, J P, and McNeill, T E, *The archaeology of Ulster* (Belfast, 1991), 69–71.

Fig. 32 Cross-incised boulder at Dunteige.

7. BEAGHMORE Stone circles, alignments and cairns Co Tyrone H 685842

13.6 km NW of Cookstown, approached either from the A505 Cookstown to Omagh road via Dunnamore or from the Draperstown to Sheskinshule minor road.

Fig. 33 Aerial view of stone circles, alignments and cairns at Beaghmore, Co Tyrone.

Beaghmore is set on the south-east fringe of the Sperrin Mountains, in uplands of bleak beauty. The site comprises a series of stone circles, rows (alignments) and cairns. It was discovered in the 1930s by George Barnett, was excavated in the 1940s, and further excavations were carried out in 1965. The peat that once shrouded the site has been cut away and a system of drainage channels prevents the monument from being reclaimed by the bog.

A sequence of human activity in this landscape has been established using pollen analysis (see *Feature 5*) linked to radiocarbon dating (see *Feature 2*). The resulting pollen diagram shows that 7,000 years ago this area was wooded, with birch, pine, willow and hazel trees. By 3500 BC grass, herb and cereal pollens begin to occur in the pollen record, so clearly the woodland had been cleared and the

land was being used for farming. The low banks of small stones that lie under the later stone monuments may be the remains of field boundaries built by the Neolithic farmers.

The stone monuments belong to the Early Bronze Age, having been constructed at some time between 1500 and 800 BC. There are three pairs of stone circles, each with a cairn set next to or between the pair. In all twelve cairns are visible, most of which were found to contain traces of cremated bones. One circle lies by itself, not forming part of a pair, completely filled with close-set stones, popularly known as 'the Dragon's Teeth'.

While we will never be certain of the exact activity that took place at Beaghmore, it does seem that four of the

Fig. 34 The 'Dragon's Teeth', Beaghmore.

stone rows point to the area on the horizon where the midsummer sunrise occurred. This suggests that the monuments were laid out in a planned manner for astronomical purposes, so perhaps the sun, moon or stars were observed, even worshipped, at this site.

After 2000 BC the climate in Europe seems to have become progressively colder and wetter. The tree-cover of this upland area in the Sperrins had been removed by the Neolithic farmers and the light soils were not suitable for prolonged agricultural use. The increased levels of rainfall now added to the problems. There were few trees to soak up the excess water through their roots and a layer of iron pan formed in the subsoil which caused the layers above to become waterlogged. The soil became more and more acidic and this killed off all the earthworms. The land became sodden and blanket peat bog grew over what had once been farmland. The peat continued to grow until eventually it swallowed up all traces of the settlements, monuments and field systems of the prehistoric inhabitants of Beaghmore.

This impressive site provides a clear example of the lack of continuity, resulting here from ecological change and human impact on the land. It took the ever-watchful eye of George Barnett in the 1930s to detect the presence of stones in the bog and the whole story is not yet uncovered. Stone features continue under the uncut bog at Beaghmore, and elsewhere in the peat other prehistoric features remain to be found and investigated.

Other stone circles include Ballynoe, Co Down (J 481404) and (in this chapter) Drumskinny, Co Fermanagh (H 201707).

Evans, E E, 'George Barnett: an appreciation', *Ulster J Archaeol* 29 (1966), 1-5; Pilcher, J R, 'Archaeology, palaeoecology and radio-carbon dating of the Beaghmore stone circle site', *Ulster J Archaeol* 32 (1969), 73-91; Burl, A, *The stone circles of the British Isles* (London, 1976); *Beaghmore stone circles and alignments* (Belfast, 1977), DOE NI guide-card; Brannon, N F, 'An excavation at Bradley's Cairn, Beaghmore townland, Co Tyrone', *Ulster J Archaeol* 42 (1979), 20-22; Thom, A S, 'The stone rings of Beaghmore: geometry and astronomy', *Ulster J Archaeol* 43 (1980), 15-19; Ó Nualláin, S, *Stone circles in Ireland* (Dublin, 1995). Further information on aspects of Bronze Age Ireland can be found in *Ireland in the Bronze Age: proceedings of the Dublin conference, April, 1995,* ed Waddell, J, and Shee-Twohig, E, (Dublin, 1995) and *Archaeology Ireland* 9.1 (1995), 'The Bronze Age issue'.

8. DRUMSKINNY | Stone circle, cairn and alignment   Co Fermanagh | H 201707

7.2 km N of Kesh, reached from the narrow minor road leading N to Castlederg.

Fig. 35 The cairn at Drumskinny, Co Fermanagh, during excavation in 1962.

Drumskinny is another example of a stone circle complex belonging to the mid-Ulster (north Fermanagh – south Londonderry – Tyrone) series. The monument is easily accessible from a roadside car-park and is probably an outlier of a group of megalithic monuments located 1.5 km to the south in Montiaghroe townland.

The site lies in an area of what is today shallow upland bog. The stone circle was visibly protruding from the surrounding blanket bog in 1934 when it was taken into State Care. It was not until excavations were carried in 1962 in advance of improvements planned for the site that the hidden complexity of the monument was

realised, for when the peat deposits were removed down to natural boulder clay further elements were revealed.

Drumskinny is a miniature version of Beaghmore, consisting of a single stone circle with accompanying cairn and alignment. The stone circle originally had 39 standing stone uprights, seven of which had later been removed. After the excavation new stones were placed in the empty socket holes of the seven missing uprights, marked MOF (for Ministry of Finance) to distinguish them from the original stones. None of the stones was more than 2 m high and the diameter of the circle was 12.8 m.

Fig. 36 Drumskinny stone circle, alignment and cairn.

Three possible gaps were identified in the circuit of the circle, but we cannot say if they were originally intended as entrances into the ring. The gap in the north-west part of the circle is near to a stone cairn, unknown before the excavation since it lay hidden under peat and whin bushes. Unlike the cairns at Beaghmore, there was no evidence to suggest that cremated human bone had been deposited in the cairn. Aligned on the centre of the cairn was a second previously unknown feature, the stone alignment, a straight row of stones, originally 24 in number, running for a distance of 7.6 m south from the cairn. Few finds were recovered during the excavation, the most important being a flint hollow scraper and a sherd of Neolithic pottery. A Bronze Age date for the construction of the monument is possible but not certain. While the complex is much smaller than the one at Beaghmore, it is clear that the same care was taken in its planning and construction, no doubt for use in similar ritual activities.

Drumskinny provides a good example of how in the absence of excavation archaeologists can never know the full scale of a monument lying largely smothered in upland bog. The factors which led to the growth of blanket bog at Creggandevesky (see Chapter 3) and Beaghmore (see this chapter) were probably the same as those responsible for its growth at Drumskinny. The growth of blanket bog was not an isolated event restricted to a single area; it was experienced throughout Ireland, occurring at different times in different areas. Three thousand years later, there is now concern in Ireland as a whole over disappearing bogland and worldwide concern about climatic change resulting from our use and abuse of the environment. It is sobering to realise that similar problems have affected people in the distant past.

Waterman, D M, 'The stone circle, cairn, and alignment at Drumskinny, Co Fermanagh', *Ulster J Archaeol* 27 (1964), 23–30.

FEATURE 5 POLLEN ANALYSIS

Pollen analysis is a method of studying past changes in vegetation. Pollen grains are very small particles which carry the male genetic material of flowering plants. These are released into the atmosphere in large quantities during spring and summer, as anyone who suffers from hay fever knows! The pollen in the atmosphere is obviously a reflection of the vegetation around at that time, and some of this falls as 'pollen rain' on the surface of lakes and peat bogs. The outer layers of pollen grains are remarkably resistant to decay and are normally well preserved in the sediments of lakes or peat bogs as these accumulate through time.

As the outer layer of the pollen grain has a shape and a surface pattern which is unique to a species or family of plants, a record of changes in the vegetation around a particular lake or peat bog is preserved. This normally only covers the period since the end of the last Ice Age in the British Isles, a period of about 13,000 years, but in areas which were not covered by ice, particularly around the Mediterranean, continuous sequences of over 100,000 years can occur.

Once an area for study has been selected, for instance the peat deposits around Beaghmore (in this chapter) or a lake like Loughnashade, near Navan Fort, Co Armagh (see Chapter 5), a sediment core is extracted. This is a continuous profile of sediment accumulated at a single point in the lake or bog. Sub-samples are taken from the core at intervals

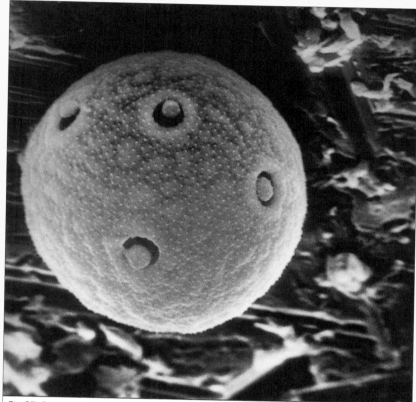

Fig. 37 Scanning electron micrograph of a pollen grain of ribwort plantain magnified 2400 times (Jonathan Pilcher).

across the time-period the pollen analyst is studying. The sediment matrix is removed using a combination of chemicals to which the pollen grains are resistant, and sieved to remove particles which are larger or smaller than the pollen grains. The remaining material is then mounted on slides and examined under a high-powered microscope. The pollen grains are identified to the level of plant species, family or type (which contains several species with similar pollen grains) and the number of each is recorded, along

with the number of charcoal particles seen.

When this process has been repeated for each sample a pollen diagram is constructed, conventionally with the oldest samples at the base of the diagram. The frequency of each pollen type is normally presented as a percentage of the total number of pollen grains from dry-land plants. This allows a graphic picture of how the vegetation has changed through time to be presented, and the profile is often dated by radiocarbon (see

Feature 2) to provide an independent chronology for these changes.

A typical pollen diagram from Ireland covering the last 13,000 years will show changes from Late-glacial grasslands through to the development of Post-glacial forests. From about 5,000 years ago the impact of humans on the landscape becomes more obvious as forests are cleared for agriculture. This results in decreases in the amounts of pollen from trees and an increase in pollen of grasses, weeds and cereals. The presence of charcoal may indicate human use of fire. Abandonment of farmland may result in regeneration of woodland, seen as an increase in tree pollen at the expense of pollen from open-ground plants. Periods of expansion and contraction of agriculture can be traced through time at a site. The results from a number of sites across a larger area, if well enough dated, can lead to the identification of periods of population increase or decrease if these events are found to occur at the same time. In Ireland such fluctuations appear to happen until the early centuries AD, when a general increase in agriculture, particularly arable farming, is evident. Pollen from lakes can reveal the pattern of agricultural changes up to the present day, including the growing of flax and even hemp, as at Loughnashade in the 17th century.

The summarized pollen diagram in Figure 39 was constructed by David Weir from pollen cores obtained at Loughnashade (see Chapter 5: Navan Fort) and it covers the period from about 4000 BC to AD 1000. Several periods of forest expansion and contraction can be seen, beginning with forest clearance in the

Fig. 38 Scanning electron micrograph of a pollen grain of hawkweed magnified 2300 times (Jonathan Pilcher).

earlier Bronze Age (episode 1) and intense forest clearance and burning during the Late Bronze Age (episode 2), during which time the hillfort called Haughey's Fort was constructed (see Chapter 5: Navan Fort). Agriculture during this period was a mixed arable/pastoral economy, shown by the discovery of large quantities of carbonized cereals (barley) and animal bones at Haughey's Fort.

Following a period with some decrease in human activity, clear from an increase in tree pollen (episode 3), the period of the Late Bronze Age / Early Iron Age transition sees a much more open land-scape with little cereal pollen present (episode 4). This suggests a primarily pastoral economy. A quite substantial period of forest regeneration occurs between 100 BC and AD 300 (episode 5) suggesting a reduction in population – a feature that is seen for this period in many other Irish pollen diagrams, including those recently constructed for pollen profiles from Co Louth. A major and sustained period of forest clearance and agriculture follows (episodes 6 and 7). The cereal pollen values are among the highest in the British Isles and show that during the Early Christian period the area's good-quality soils were being used mainly for arable farming.

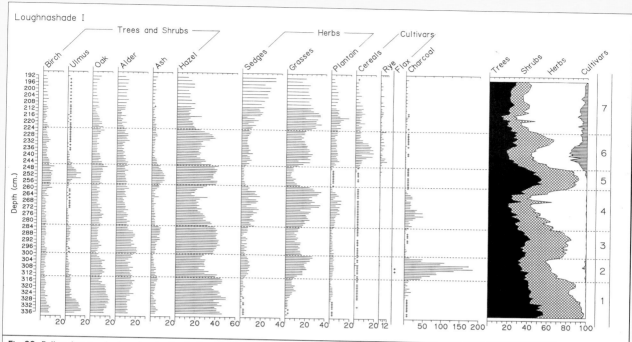

Fig. 39 Pollen diagram for Loughnashade, Co Armagh, showing seven main episodes of vegetation change (David Weir).

Weir, D A, 'Palynology and the environmental history of the Navan area: a preliminary study', *Emania* 3 (1987), 34-43; Pilcher, J R, *Palaeoecology: an introduction to the study of past environments* (Belfast, 1988); Moore, P D, Webb, J A, and Collinson, M E, *Pollen analysis* (London, 1991); Weir, D A, 'The environment of Emain Macha', *Ulidia: proceedings of the first international conference on the Ulster Cycle of Tales* (Belfast, 1994), ed Mallory, J P, and Stockman, G, 171-79; Mitchell, F, and Ryan, M, *Reading the Irish landscape*, third edition (Dublin, 1997).

Fig. 40 Navan Fort, Co Armagh (Infra-red photograph by Tony Corey).

Chapter 5

The Heroic Age

3.2 km W of Armagh, reached from a by-road north of the A28 to Killylea. The Navan Centre opened in 1993. This project combines educational and cultural displays with full facilities including a large car-park approached from the A28.

Navan Fort is widely regarded as the premier archaeological monument in Northern Ireland. The monument stands on a small, grassy drumlin and is a large, circular earthwork enclosure. The earthwork has a diameter of 250 m and consists of a large bank (best preserved on its west and south sides) set immediately downslope from a ditch. An entrance on the north-west leads to the summit of the encircled hilltop. On a clear day the view of the surrounding countryside is extensive, especially to the north. The tower and steeples of the two cathedrals in Armagh City can be seen to the east.

At the base of the eastern slope of the hill lies a small lake, Loughnashade. The area between the hilltop enclosure and Loughnashade is occupied by a disused quarry filled with water. It is hoped that at some time in the future the quarry site will be 'landscaped' (for safety reasons visitors are not alowed to go outside the monument's perimeter fence facing the quarry). Two archaeological features can be seen on the summit of the drumlin. The first is a low circular platform with a surrounding infilled ditch. The second is a large grassy mound, 6 m high and 60 m in diameter.

Although called a 'fort', it is unlikely that the Navan enclosure was a fortification in prehistoric times. An outer bank and an inner ditch will not provide defensive strength; in fact it gives the advantage to attackers. They can climb to the top of the bank and strike down at defenders in the ditch. The enclosing bank and ditch at Navan have never been excavated, but the arrangement of bank and ditch is similar to that of Late Neolithic ceremonial henges, such as the Giant's Ring, Ballynahatty, Co Down (see Chapter 3). A soil core for pollen analysis (see *Feature 5*) taken from the silted-up ditch by David Weir provided material for a radiocarbon date (see *Feature 2*) which suggested that the ditch had been constructed before *circa* 550 BC. Future excavation may show that the bank and ditch belong to the Neolithic period and that the monument was originally constructed as a 'henge', but other dates are possible.

Between 1961 and 1971 Dudley Waterman carried out a series of excavations on the two monuments on the summit of the hill. Under the smaller mound he found evidence of Neolithic activity in the form of pottery, flint and ploughmarks. There was no clear evidence for

Fig. 41 Navan Fort, Co Armagh, from the air with quarry edge in foreground.

the date of the circular ditched monument, but it is possible that it was an Iron Age ring-barrow, a form of burial mound. The most remarkable discoveries were made at the larger mound. During the Late Bronze Age, around 700 BC, a circular ditched and fenced enclosure was built in the area now covered by this mound. Later a wooden house, yard and fenced droveway were built. The house was rebuilt eleven times during the Early Iron Age (*circa* 300 to 100 BC). This indicates that the site was regarded as important over a very long period in prehistoric times. The aristocratic nature of this activity was highlighted by the discovery of the skull of a Barbary ape in one of the wall foundation trenches. The context in which the skull was found, and a radio-carbon date obtained from a sample of the bone, indicate that the animal had lived at the site during the 2nd century BC. Clearly, whoever resided here had connections with north Africa and the Mediterranean area during the Iron Age.

In the 1st century BC the structures were cleared and a complex and time-consuming series of ritual activities took place. A huge, circular wooden construction was raised, 40 m in diameter, with five rings of oak posts (275 in all) carefully aligned around a large central post. The stump of the central post survived and, using dendrochronology (see *Feature* 7), it dated the erection of the structure to 95 BC. There was evidence to show that some form of superstructure was placed on top of the posts, but this was not necessarily a roof. Soon after, while the timber structure was still standing, it was filled with limestone blocks to form a cairn 3 m high and the whole structure was set ablaze. Finally a deep deposit of clay and sods was placed over the surface of the cairn to form the high mound which the visitor sees today.

The whole sequence of events seems to have been planned and initiated with the purpose of constructing and burning what has been described by some as a

Fig. 42 Navan Fort: Iron Age enclosures discovered during excavation of the large mound (Site B) in 1967.

Fig. 43 Navan Fort: limestone cairn revealed during the excavation of the large mound (Site B) in 1965.

wooden temple. The religious leaders of Iron Age society – the druids – must have planned and orchestrated the events. Perhaps they sacrificed this composite structure though a holocaust rite to the Celtic gods and goddesses. Certainly Navan must have been a major religious centre.

Archaeological research has shown that Navan Fort was not an isolated monument in the landscape, and the surrounding district contains a number of other important monuments. Four bronze trumpets of the 1st century BC were found in boggy ground at the edge of Loughnashade (H 852454) in the late 18th century. Several human skulls and animal bones were found in the vicinity of the trumpets. The Celts are known to have made sacrifices to their deities by placing offerings in watery locations, and Loughnashade was probably a sacred lake. One kilometre to the west is the King's Stables (H 838454), a Late Bronze Age artifical pond probably used for ritual purposes. Animal bones and the facial part of a human skull were discovered at the bottom of this pool during an excavation by Chris Lynn in 1975, so the King's Stables would seem to have been another sacred 'lake'. On a hill to the west of the King's Stables is Haughey's Fort (H 835452), a Late Bronze Age hillfort recently excavated by Jim Mallory. In the townland of Ballyrea (H 845448) an Early Christian period linear ditch, possibly a field boundary, was discovered in 1992 in advance of the construction of the Navan Centre. The profusion and variety of monuments found within the Navan landscape indicates that this was an area of major significance throughout prehistoric times, and that its former status cast a shadow into the historic period. Navan Fort's Irish name, *Emain Macha*, later *Eamhain Mhacha*, can be translated as 'twins of Macha'. Macha was a goddess associated with the region who also lent her name to the later ecclesiastical settlement of Armagh, *Ard Macha*, 'the Hill of Macha'. Early Irish legend provides stories of how *Eamhain Mhacha* received its name, but it seems that some of these tales may have been developed by Early Christian authors who knew little about the goddess except her name. Some of the legends about the site may, however, contain an element of tradition inherited from the pagan past.

The first historical reference to the site is probably in a 2nd-century AD gazetteer of Ireland compiled by the Greek geographer Ptolemy. Two important places are located in Ulster, *Regia* or 'royal place' and *Isamnion*. While it is possible that either place may be Navan, the latter seems the more likely candidate on linguistic grounds. The modern name 'Navan' derives from either *An Eamhain* or *i n-Eamhain*, 'in Emain'. Navan Fort is firmly identified with *Eamhain Mhacha* of Early Irish narratives, the ancient capital of the people of Ulster. This was the home of their king, Conchobhar, the warrior Cú Chulainn, the tragic Deirdre, Cathbhadh the druid and the Red Branch warriors in a group of stories now known as the Ulster Cycle. Described as Europe's oldest vernacular literature, the Ulster Cycle tells of the great events that occurred at *Eamhain Mhacha*, and of the heroic battles fought against Queen Meadhbh and the people of Connaught. The sagas have an enduring importance and have provided inspiration for writers, artists and musicians, but how does the

Fig. 44 Navan Fort: large mound (Site B) restored after excavation.

content of this early Irish literature relate to the archae-ological evidence?

The fictitious 'prehistoric' sections of the early Irish Annals assign the events of the Ulster Cycle to the 1st centuries BC and AD, but the tales were first written down by Christian monks in the 7th or 8th centuries AD. The Iron Age structures revealed by archaeological exca-vation at Navan Fort may not directly relate to the Early Christian literary descriptions of *Eamhain Mhacha*, but the sagas do mark the site as the capital of a kingdom which held sway here around the time of the birth of Christ. The archaeological record provides independent evidence that Navan Fort was indeed both a high status settlement and a major ceremonial centre during the period when the early Irish annals indicate that the site was at the height of its power. Forces other than coincidence must surely be at play here. It is highly probable that an oral tradition with origins in prehistory identified the earthworks at Navan Fort as a place of authority, and that this tradition was transmitted into the Early Christian literature. The

material culture depicted in the tales, however, does not tally with our knowledge of Iron Age weapons or jewellery. The evidence suggests that the early sagas may have been fleshed out with the material culture of the Early Christian period but that the monks were consciously attempting to portray a past world. In doing so they may have married folk recollections, oral tales and interpretations of the landscape with the material culture of their own time, and in the process preserved some real information about how the site was perceived and used in prehistory.

It is traditionally believed that Navan was abandoned as the capital of Ulster in the 4th century AD when the Airghialla forced the Ulster people eastwards, but the establishment of an ecclesiastical settlement at nearby Armagh in the 5th century AD suggests that the area surrounding Navan was still an important religious, if not political, focal point. References to the abandoned capital are found in the Irish Annals, but by historic times it had become a landmark and a symbol of the past. In the medieval period, as late as 1387, the Ulster king, Niall O'Neill, built a house at Navan to entertain poets and scholars, probably motivated by a desire to associate himself with the capital of Ulster's past rulers. A pictorial map of Armagh drawn by Richard Bartlett in 1602 shows the deserted Navan earthworks with Loughnashade in the distance.

The limestone quarry to the east of the monument had its origins in the 19th century, but the quarry only reached its present size in the 1970s. After a Public Inquiry in 1985 the Department of the Environment withdrew permission for continued quarrying and a charitable trust, Navan at Armagh, was set up with the aim of protecting and promoting the monument and its landscape to a wider audience. The Navan Centre is the product of their work. A second organisation, the Navan Research Group, was founded in 1986 and it is concerned with furthering knowledge of Navan, the surrounding archaeological landscape, the Early Irish literature and the Iron Age. The results of these studies are published in the journal *Emania*.

Navan Fort and its landscape display a wealth of evidence both for continuity and for change throughout the ages. Navan's history runs from Neolithic beginnings to Late Bronze Age settlement and ritual, and from Iron Age ceremonial centre to abandoned capital in the shadow of the new religious centre in Armagh. In the Early Christian period and medieval times it was remembered as the home of kings and heroes, and the setting for numerous legendary deeds – the ancient capital of Ulster.

Lynn, C J, 'Trial excavations at the King's Stables, Tray townland, County Armagh', *Ulster J Archaeol* 40 (1977), 42-62; Lynn, C J, 'Navan Fort – a draft summary account of D M Waterman's excavations', *Emania* 1 (1986), 11-19; Mallory, J P, *Navan Fort - the ancient capital of Ulster* (Belfast, 1987); *Navan Fort (Emain Macha)* (Belfast, 1987), DOE NI guide-card; Lynn, C J, *Pieces of the past* (HMSO, Belfast, 1988), ed Hamlin, A, and Lynn, C J, 19-21; Simpson, D A A, 'Neolithic Navan?', *Emania* 6 (1989), 31-3; Weir, D A, 'A radiocarbon date from the Navan Fort ditch', *Emania* 6 (1989), 34-5; Mallory, J P, 'Further dates from Haughey's Fort', *Emania* 9 (1991), 64-5; Crothers, N, 'Further excavations at Ballyrea townland, Co Armagh', *Emania* 11 (1993), 49-54; Lynn, C J, 'Navan Fort – home of gods and goddesses?', *Archaeology Ireland* 7.1 (1993), 17-21; Mallory, J P, 'The world of Cú Chulainn: the archaeology of *Táin Bó Cúailnge*', *Aspects of the Táin* (Belfast, 1993), ed Mallory, J P, 103-59; Lynn, C J, 'Hostels, heroes and tales: further thoughts on the Navan mound', *Emania* 12 (1994), 5-20; Mallory, J P, 'Haughey's Fort – Macha's other twin?', *Archaeology Ireland* 9.1 (1995), 28-30; Waterman, D M, *Excavations in Navan Fort, County Armagh, 1961-1971* (Belfast, 1997), Northern Ireland Archaeological Monographs: No 3, completed and edited by Lynn, C J.

10. THE DORSEY RAMPARTS · Linear earthworks · Co Armagh · Between H 936190 and J 955197

2 km NW of Silver Bridge along the A29 road from Newtownhamilton to Dundalk.

The Dorsey ramparts constitute an 'enclosure' made up of a series of large linear earthworks, some 4 km in circumference. The earthworks enclose an area of bogland and rough terrain lying between a series of drumlins and small lakes to the west and the Slieve Gullion mountain range to the east. The Dorsey stands in the path of the easiest route of travel either north into the Armagh plains or south into Louth. The name 'Dorsey' comes from the Irish plural *Doirse*, meaning 'doors' or 'gates', and the monument probably acted as a defensive line where movement into and out of Ulster could be controlled. Although much of the irregular circuit of the enclosure has been destroyed, the visitor can imagine something of the original shape and size of the ramparts from viewing two surviving sections of the more southerly rampart line (H 942189 and H 953193).

The southern rampart has a central bank with a deep ditch on either side, the top of the bank standing 8 m higher than the bottom of the ditch. Only slight traces now remain of the northern rampart but it seems to have been a less formidable defence, having only a bank and single ditch.

In 1977 a section of the northern rampart was excavated. A layer of charcoal and burnt soil was identified as the remains of a timber palisade which had been covered over by the rampart bank immediately after it had burned down. Charcoal samples from the layer were sent for radiocarbon dating (see *Feature 2*) and this revealed that the timbers used in the palisade had grown at some time between the years 380 BC and AD 25, indicating an Iron Age date for the structure.

Fig. 45 The Dorsey Ramparts, Co Armagh: aerial view of southern rampart, visible in top left of photograph.

Also in 1977 a number of large oak timbers were discovered in a bog on the line of a section of the southern rampart. The timbers were part of a palisade set in a shallow bedding trench across wet ground. The line of the bedding trench was traced for some 60 m and it was shown that it ran parallel to and inside the rampart ditch. The oak timbers were submitted for dendrochronological dating (see *Feature 7*) and this showed that the timbers used in the construction of the palisade had been cut down in about 100 BC - almost the same date as that of the large central timber post from the multi-ring structure at Navan Fort (see this chapter). It seems probable that there is a connection between the Dorsey and the political or religious power that occupied Navan Fort, 27 km to the north. This population group may have undertaken the construction of the southern line of the Dorsey ramparts to provide defence against attacks launched into their heartlands in the Armagh plains. Alternatively, the monument may have been erected by the Iron Age inhabitants of Louth, either to prevent intrusions into

their territory by the northeners or as a means of controlling a primary route into the north.

It has recently been suggested by Chris Lynn that the Dorsey ramparts were not constructed as an enclosure but that the 'monument' is made up of two lines of ramparts built at different periods. The earthworks only resemble an enclosure because an earlier, slighter (northern) line was supplemented by a far more substantial (southern) rampart in about 100 BC. This theory gained supporting evidence in 1988, when further oak posts were discovered along the northern line of earthworks. The posts were dendrochronologically dated and were found to be to some 50 years earlier than the timbers recovered from the southern ramparts in 1977.

The Dorsey may have been part of a much more extensive larger defensive line that ran from Co Donegal to Co Monaghan, called the Black Pig's Dyke. This is not a continuous earthwork running across the entire southern

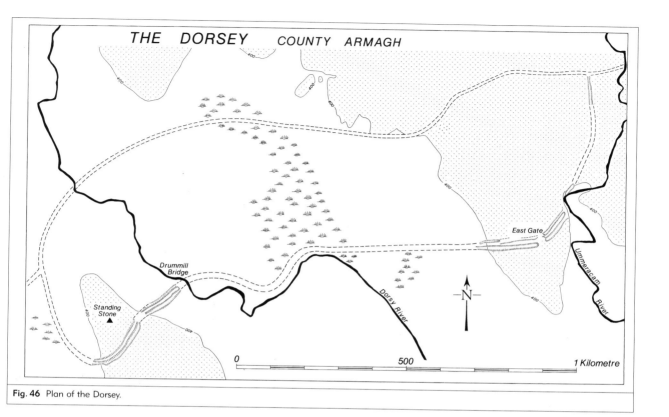

Fig. 46 Plan of the Dorsey.

border of Ulster but is found in those areas where the landscape does not provide natural protection in the form of lakes or high ground. Excavations by Aidan Walsh at a section of this earthwork in Co Monaghan showed it to be of a similar date to the Dorsey ramparts, but only further archaeological research could show whether the entire length of the Black Pig's Dyke was built during one period of activity in prehistoric times. There could be some link also with a linear earthwork called the Dane's Cast, which runs north-south in west Co Down. This is particularly clear in the Scarva area, but it has not been excavated so its date is unknown. The study of linear earthworks in Ireland is still in its infancy, but other examples are known, such as the 'Doon' of Drumsna in Co Roscommon and *an Cladh Ruadh* in Co Kerry. Linear earthworks may have been used by Iron Age peoples to delimit territory between kingdoms. Although we are still puzzled by these monuments, we can be fairly sure that the lines now drawn in ink to identify boundaries between district councils, counties and countries some-

times have their origins more than two thousand years ago in earthworks like the Dorsey ramparts.

Tempest, H G, 'The Dorsey', *County Louth Archaeological Journal* 6.2 (1930), 187-240; Lynn, C J, 'The Dorsey and other linear earthworks', *Studies on early Ireland: essays in honour of M V Duignan* (Belfast, 1980), ed Scott, B G, 121-8; Lynn, C J, *Pieces of the past* (HMSO, Belfast, 1988), ed Hamlin, A, and Lynn, C J, 21-4; Baille, M G L, and Brown, D M, 'Further dates from the Dorsey', *Emania* 6 (1989), 11; Buckley, V M, 'From the darkness to the dawn: the later prehistoric and Early Christian border-lands', *The borderlands: essays on the history of the Ulster-Leinster border* (Belfast, 1989), ed Gillespie, R, and O'Sullivan, H, 23-39; Lynn, C J, 'An interpretation of the Dorsey', *Emania* 6 (1989), 5-10; Lynn, C J, 'Excavations at the Dorsey, County Armagh, 1977', *Ulster J Archaeol* 54-55 (1991-92), 61-77.

FEATURE 6 THE CELTS

Fig. 47 The Boa Island figure, Co Fermanagh.

'Celtic' is a linguistic term used to describe a group of languages known to have have been spoken during the 1st millennium BC in Europe. Celtic languages have their origins in an ancestor language – Indo-European – thought to have been spoken 4,500 years ago. Gaulish, Lepontic and Celtiberian are examples of Celtic languages once in use in Europe but now extinct, each having been replaced by a Latin-based language. By the 7th century AD Celtic languages continued to be spoken only in north-west Europe, and these

languages were Irish, Scots Gaelic, Manx, Welsh, Cornish and Breton. The increased use of English as the main language of the British Isles brought the Celtic languages near to extinction during historic times. Today only Irish, Welsh, Scots Gaelic and Breton survive to any significant extent, although attempts are being made to revive Manx and Cornish.

Archaeologists tend to be cautious about using a linguistic term, but the word 'Celtic' is sometimes applied to two archaeological

cultural phases in prehistoric Europe when Celtic languages may have been spoken. The two cultures originated in central Europe and evolved at the same time as iron technology was developing. They both applied a distinctive abstract, swirling type of decoration to their jewellery, weapons and religious objects. The earlier phase is called 'Hallstatt', after a salt-mining settlement discovered near an Austrian lake in the 19th century. This phase probably began during the Late Bronze Age, around 1200 BC, and

Fig. 48 The Derrykeighan Stone, Co Antrim (Ulster Museum).

continued into the Iron Age, ending in the mid 5th century BC. The second phase started around 500 BC and is named 'La Tène' after a settlement found in Switzerland in 1858. This phase continued until the expansion of the Roman Empire into the Celtic homelands from the 2nd century BC onwards. After the conquest of Britain (initiated by the Emperor Claudius in AD 43) the tribes living in Scotland and Ireland were the only insular Celts who remained outside the Roman Empire.

The name 'Celt' has its origins in the works of the writers of ancient Greece and Rome. From the 5th century BC onwards it was used as a general term for the barbarian tribes who lived to the north of the Mediterranean area. In the texts the Celts were described as a tall, fair-haired people, strong but vain, who enjoyed alcohol and warfare and were very superstitious. They were generally good natured but prone to mood-swings that saw them melancholic one moment and in a ferocious temper the next. Celtic society

was ruled by an aristocratic élite with a priestly class, the druids, who acted as philosophers, teachers and judges. Such descriptions, however, can only be sweeping generalisations. The Celtic-speaking tribes lived over a wide geographical area and it is likely that they represented a wide variety of peoples and types.

The earliest examples of the Irish language in Ireland date from the 4th or 5th centuries AD in the form of inscriptions on stones in the script called ogham. It is generally agreed that a Celtic language was introduced at some time after the end of the Late Bronze Age, around 1200 BC, but before the 2nd century AD. Exactly how and when, however, is a matter of debate. At around 700 BC Hallstatt types of material, primarily swords, begin to appear in Ireland. We might view this as evidence for a movement of Celtic-speaking people into Ireland, but the objects are fashioned in bronze and not in iron, and the swords may simply be products of native craftworkers making bronze copies of Continental iron swords. By 300 BC the first La Tène-decorated artifacts are identified in the archaeological record, with a second phase of La Tène material appearing around 100 BC. Can the movement of Continentally-inspired La Tène material in either of these phases be taken as evidence that new people were moving into Ireland? A number of leading archaeologists do not think so. They argue that the La Tène art-styles could have been adopted by native craftworkers and that population movement was not necessarily involved. What other archaeological evidence exists which might shed light on this period and the appearance of a Celtic language in Ireland?

Except for a few sites like Navan Fort and the Dorsey ramparts (see this chapter) the evidence for Iron Age settlement in Ireland is very scarce. Burial evidence is also limited to a small number of sites, including the 21 cremated burials surrounding a Neolithic passage tomb at Kiltierney, Co Fermanagh. A number of carved stones are considered to be of Iron Age date. One example in Caldragh Graveyard on Boa Island, Co Fermanagh, may date from the 1st century BC or AD, though a date

in the Early Christian period has also been suggested. It is a stone 'idol' with two figures, back-to-back, each with a large head and crossed limbs. A stone from Derrykeighan graveyard, Co Antrim, (now housed in the Ulster Museum) is decorated with accomplished flowing La Tène forms. The tally of Iron Age material from Ireland, however, is still very meagre.

Although weapons and jewellery fashioned using the new metalworking techniques and decorated with 'Celtic' art styles show that changes did occur in Ireland during this period, this material in itself is not sufficent evidence to prove that Celtic-speaking tribes migrated into Ireland. The fact remains, however, that a Celtic language was the dominant tongue in this island by the dawn of the Early Christian period. This did not happen without some catalyst having created the conditions needed for change to occur, and population movement remains a very strong candidate to explain how this change came about. We know from Julius Caesar that the Celts undertook mass migrations. He describes the attempts of a tribe called the Helvetii to migrate from Switzerland to the west coast of southern Gaul in 58 BC. There is clear archaeological evidence that people from Gaul settled in parts of Yorkshire and southern England in the 1st century BC, and Celtic-speaking peoples may have come into Ireland in one or more similar migrations.

Any new arrivals would have found themselves greatly outnumbered by the people already living in Ireland, but who were these people? Many must have been the descendants of the builders of the megalithic tombs

and other monuments discussed in Chapters 3 and 4. There may have been groups of earlier incomers, difficult or impossible to detect in the archaeological record. Why the pre-Celtic population of Ireland abandoned its own language and adopted what emerged as Irish is not clearly understood. Perhaps powerful newcomers established their Celtic tongue as the language of social and economic contacts and the 'native' peoples saw that it was to their advantage to make the change.

Tierney, J J, 'The Celtic ethnography of Posidonius', *PRIA*, Section C, 60 (1960), 189-275; Ross, A, *Pagan Celtic Britain* (London, 1967); Ross, A, *The pagan Celts* (London, 1970); Powell, T G E, *The Celts* (London, 1980); Foley, C, *Pieces of the past* (HMSO, Belfast, 1988), ed Hamlin, A, and Lynn, C J, 24-6; Megaw, R, and V, *Celtic art* (London, 1989); Mallory, J P, and McNeill, T E, *The archaeology of Ulster* (Belfast, 1991), 140-79; Kruta, V, Frey, O H, Raftery, B, and Szabó, M, (ed) *The Celts* (London, 1991); Green, M, (ed) *The Celtic world* (London, 1995). Six articles expressing a variety of considered views on the question of the origins of the Irish language can be found in *Emania* 9 (1991).

FEATURE 7 DENDROCHRONOLOGY

Fig. 49 Sampling an oak timber (Mike Baillie).

It is a commonly known fact that each year most trees produce a ring of new wood under their bark. The tree-rings accumulate over the years so that when a tree is felled the circles of growth can be counted to give a measure of its age, and their relative widths record the tree's response to changing environmental conditions.

Dendrochronology is a dating method based on this natural process. The dendrochronologist measures and plots the widths of all the rings in a sample of wood to provide a ring pattern for an individual tree. The ring patterns of successively older trees of the same species in the same region are then collected, overlapped and cross-matched. As the samples build up, going progressively further backwards in time, a long continuous sequence of tree-rings from many different trees is created reaching back over hundreds and eventually thousands of years.

In Northern Ireland this work has been pioneered by Mike Baillie and his colleagues in the Palaeoecology Centre at the Queen's University of Belfast. Their research began in 1968 and the dendrochronological calendar was completed back to 5289 BC in 1984. The concept of dendrochronology may seem to be simple, but in Mike Baillie's own words the work 'can be extremely difficult, time-consuming and frustrating'.

The Belfast team used Irish oak trees to build up their calendar because

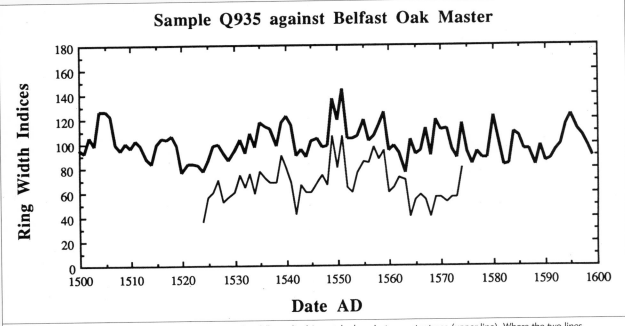

Fig. 50 How dendrochronology works. The sample to be dated (lower line) is matched against a master trace (upper line). Where the two lines correspond, a time span is identified and the age of the sample is revealed (Mike Baillie).

oak was known to have been used in prehistoric and historic times in Ireland, while other wood types such as elm and ash were rarely used in buildings before the 17th century. The continuous presence of oak from all periods made this species the best candidate to push far back into the past. A further reason for choosing oak was that large quantities of this species are preserved as sub-fossil 'bog-oaks' in peat bogs. This meant that if the historic section of the sequence could be established then the prehistoric section would suffer from no shortage of timber.

Starting from standing oak trees, then working back into the past, samples were obtained from oak timbers in historic buildings such as Hillsborough Fort (see Chapter 11). Medieval timbers found during excavations at Dublin and Drogheda provided samples for the next section of the sequence. From the Early Christian period the oak beams used in the construction of crannogs and horizontal mills yielded samples that extended the chronology back to the 1st century AD. A difficult gap in the 1st centuries BC was filled by oaks from Roman Carlisle and the great central oak post from Navan Fort, datable to 94 BC (see this chapter). The 'bog-oaks' allowed the sequence to be taken back far into prehistory, and the present dendrochronological calendar stretches back beyond 5400 BC. The Northern Ireland oak chronology does not stand in isolation. It has now been successfully matched with an independent sequence from Germany dating back to 7200 BC to produce a reliable north European tree-ring chronology. These chronologies have, in turn, allowed the dating of a continuous English oak series back to 5000 BC.

If an object of oak with more than 100 growth rings is recovered during an excavation its tree-ring pattern can be measured and cross-matched against the master chronological sequence using both computer comparisons and human judgement. If successful, the exact date of the last growth ring can be determined and, if sapwood is present, the exact felling date established. A recent example of dendrochronological dating in action is the Neolithic date of 2739 BC given to a piece of oak, perhaps the remains of a log-boat, found in October 1991 during dredging operations in the river Quoile in Co Down.

It would obviously be convenient if everyone in the past had used oak when building houses or boats, but nfortunately this was not the case. The Belfast dendrochronological alendar can only be used to date bjects made of oak and not arte-acts made from any other kind of vood. It has, however, come to the id of another major dating tech-ique employed by archaeologists, y providing precisely-dated wood amples to calibrate (fine-tune) adiocarbon dates (see *Feature 2*). Jsing the resulting calibration urves allows 'raw' radiocarbon ates to be converted to estimates of eal age.

he most recent advance in dendrochronology has arisen from he recognition that tree-rings ecord environmental changes that have happened in the past. When a large volcano erupts in the Mediterranean, for instance, dust is thrown into the atmosphere and volcanic gases are released. This leads to sunlight being reflected back from the earth, and it appears that a colder, wetter climate is then experi-enced in the northern hemisphere. Vegetation in Ireland would suffer in the following years from restricted growth, and this is recorded in the tree-ring record as a succession of narrow rings. The research initiated by Mike Baillie and Martin Munroe is still in its infancy, but already there is convincing evidence of a correla-tion between entries in the early Irish annals detailing plagues and famines for particular years and sequences of stunted growth rings on the master chronology for the same years, both possibly caused by the same external natural forces.

Baillie, M G L, *Tree-ring dating and archae-ology* (London, 1982); Baillie, M G L, 'Irish dendrochronology and radio-carbon calibration', *Ulster J Archaeol* 48 (1985), 11-23; Baillie, M G L, 'Irish oaks record volcanic dust veils drama!', *Archaeology Ireland* 2.2 (1988), 71-4; Aitken, M J, *Science-based dating in archae-ology* (Harlow, 1990), 36-49; Baillie, M G L, 'Marking in marker dates: towards an archaeology with historical precision', *World Archaeology* 23.2 (1991), 233-43; Renfrew, C, and Bahn, P, *Archaeology: theories, methods and practice* (London, 1991), 118-21; Baillie, M G L, *A Slice through time: dendrochronology and precision dating* (London, 1995).

Fig. 51 Nendrum Monastery, Co Down (Infra-red photograph by Tony Corey).

Chapter 6

The Early Christian Church

3.2 km NNW of Enniskillen. A ferry operates between Trory Point and the island from Easter to September. The car-park and ferry are reached along a winding lane from the junction of the B82 to Kesh with the A32 to Ballinamallard.

Devenish is an L-shaped island at the south end of Lower Lough Erne. Its name, *Daimhinis*, means 'ox island', and it must always have provided rich pasture. The monastery's founder and patron is St Molaise, who died in the late 6th century. Written sources indicate that it became a very important place, referred to as 'multitudinous Devenish' in about AD 800, but also that it was attacked by Vikings in 837. It was burned 'with its churches' in 1157 and another fire is recorded in 1360.

The island is now uninhabited and, approaching the monastery by water, the visitor may well wonder why such a remote place was chosen by the early monks. In the past, however, travel was often easier by water than on land through woods and bogs. Far from being remote, Devenish is near the centre of the great Erne waterway and in early times this was a bustling thoroughfare, with visitors arriving by boat for services, trade, hospitality – and for burial.

The building nearest the jetty is St Molaise's Church, a very long, narrow ruin with a domestic wing north of the church. Two features show that the west end of the church dates from the early 13th century: the bulky angle pilasters on the external corners and the fine window in the south wall with elegant continuous roll mouldings. The east end of the church is a later extension, and the Maguire chapel on the south is also an addition; two Maguire stone coats-of-arms are built into the walls. Inside St Molaise's are two stones with strange stories attached to them. The medieval stone coffin used to be part of 'St Molaise's Bed', and people used to lie in it in the hope of a cure, while the double-sided bullaun stone traditionally carried the saint over the sea. The explanation is more prosaic: the hollows were used to crush food or other materials, and bullaun stones are commonly found at early church sites. St Molaise's served as the parish church for the area in the Middle Ages, and the domestic accommodation on its north side was used by the resident clergy, known as Culdees.

Continuing up the hill, the visitor next reaches St Molaise's 'House', the remains of a small church strongly associated in tradition with the founding saint. It is notable for its thick walls, made of very large stones, and the fine decoration on the bases of its angle pilasters, clearly of the 12th century. The very thick side walls supported an all-stone roof which was intact until the

Fig. 52 Aerial view of Devenish, Co Fermanagh.

early 19th century, when the building was quarried for stone and the roof collapsed. Surviving roofing stones show that they were cut to give the impression of wooden shingles, and it has been suggested that this church is a 12th-century rebuilding in stone of a greatly revered wooden church burned in the fire of 1157.

West of St Molaise's 'House' is the round tower, standing to its full height of 25 m and one of the finest in Ireland. The semicircular-headed door is 2.7 m above ground level, now approached by a modern metal stair. There are four windows just below the cap and above them is a projecting cornice with continuous decoration and a finely carved head above each of the windows. Their style points to a date in the later 12th century, and decoration of this quality on a round tower cornice in Ireland is unique. Also near the base of the cap a keen eye will see an inscription recording restoration work done by Robert Rexter in 1835. Inside, modern ladders and floors allow you to climb to the top of the tower and look out of the four windows. Devenish is one of the later round

towers. They were first built in the late 9th or early 10th centuries and it is clear that they were multi-purpose structures. Their name in Early Irish, *cloictech*, means 'bell house' and it is thought that hand bells were rung from the top windows to mark the times of services. The height of the towers would suggest that they were 'advertisements' in the landscape for the monastery, visible to travellers and a symbol of the community's affluence. The annals show that they were also used for the storage and safekeeping of precious goods, and as a refuge for people in times of trouble. The projecting stones on the inside walls may have been used for hanging bags or satchels containing precious items. The elevated door is clearly a safety feature, originally reached only by a moveable ladder. Near the round tower is the low foundation of another, perhaps earlier, round tower, found by excavation in 1973 and now built up slightly for display.

At the highest point of the hill is St Mary's Abbey (or Priory), a church of the Augustinian Canons. It is likely that the Canons were established on Devenish in the 12th

Fig. 53 Devenish: St Molaise's Church and lower graveyard.

century, but this church is clearly of the late Middle Ages. An inscription of 1449 suggests that the main fabric dates from the mid 15th century, including the finely decorated door in the north wall of the chancel, but the prominent tower, chancel arch and (reconstructed) west door are of about 1500. They are all built with grey carboniferous limestone, which became very popular in the late Middle Ages over much of Ireland. It is tempting to see the beautiful carved female head at the apex of the west door (original in the site museum) as St Mary. Notice also the small ribbed vault under the tower, the holes for bell-ropes, and the high-level doors which once led out onto a rood screen, all unusual survivals in Ulster.

North of the church is a small cloister where the canons lived, worked, ate and slept. The east range was excavated between 1972 and 1974 by Dudley Waterman and its archaeology turned out to be very complicated. The 15th-century walls overlay earlier features but these could not be closely dated. There were plentiful signs of burning – burnt wood, straw, grain and other materials – and some

of the standing masonry at the north-east corner of the cloister shows shattering by fire. Excavation also produced sherds of fine pottery from France, Germany, Spain and the Netherlands, perhaps brought by some of the travellers who stayed on Devenish on their way to the internationally famous pilgrimage island in Lough Derg, Co Donegal.

There are two graveyards on Devenish, the lower one beside St Molaise's Church and the upper graveyard south of St Mary's. There are many fine gravestones in both areas, but the upper graveyard is notable for its very unusual, intricately-carved 15th-century high cross and for a slab carved with a human figure, now reset as an upright gravestone but originally recumbent over a tomb.

From the upper graveyard it is possible to look down the slope and imagine what the early monastery may have looked like. Instead of the present stone ruins, none earlier than the 12th century, picture two or three wooden churches, communal buildings like refectory and

Fig. 54 Devenish: the round tower.

St Mary's was in ruins in the early 17th century, and parish worship was moved to Monea in the same century. Nevertheless the link with the old island site was not forgotten: in about 1800 the east window of St Mary's was moved and built into the parish church at Monea, where it can still be seen, and burial continued in the island graveyards until the 19th century. Devenish therefore presents a remarkable example of continuity, from the time of St Molaise in the 6th century. Despite the disruption of Viking attacks, damage by fire, changes in the church in the 12th century, and major changes in the church and in the population in the 15th and 16th centuries, Devenish has always been a very important place to the people of Fermanagh. The remains of the monastery have been in State Care since the Disestablishment of the Church of Ireland in 1869, and every year the peace and beauty of Devenish are enjoyed by thousands of visitors.

Other Round towers can be visited at Antrim (J 154878) and Armoy (D 078332), both in Co Antrim (see also Nendrum in this chapter). A small church of slightly later date than St Molaise's 'House' can be seen on White Island (H 175600), also in Co Fermanagh. Inishmacsaint (H 165541) is another island monastery in Lower Lough Erne.

Radford, C A R, 'Devenish', *Ulster J Archaeol* 33 (1970), 55–62; *Devenish* (Belfast, 1979), DOE NI guide-card; Hickey, H, *Images of stone: figure sculpture of the Lough Erne Basin* (Belfast, 1985); Hamlin, A, *Pieces of the past* (HMSO, Belfast, 1988), ed Hamlin, A, and Lynn, C J, 52–4.

kitchen, thatched wooden houses for the monks, workshops, barns, byres, gardens, orchards and fields. Within the line of a low bank and ditch it is still possible to see traces of small earthwork enclosures on the hillside.

12. NENDRUM	Monastery Co Down	J 524637

8.4 km S of Comber, reached by a winding road off the A22 and across causeways. Small car-park at roadside.

Nendrum monastery is on a ridge at the south-west end of Mahee Island off the western shore of Strangford Lough. Like Devenish (see this chapter), it is sited on an important early waterway and until recently could only have been reached by boat, but it is now connected to the mainland by bridges and causeways. In 1994 divers from IUART and local sports clubs (see *Feature 14*) identified a pair of low stone walls on the foreshore to the south-west of the

monastery. The walls ran downslope from the high-water mark to just below the low-water mark and sherds of 13th-century pottery were found associated with them. Both the inter-tidal location and the pottery evidence suggest that the walls were part of a harbour serving the medieval (and perhaps earlier) monastic community on the island, and that the harbour was reached by a raised path leading down from the monastery enclosure.

Fig. 55 Aerial view of Nendrum Monastery, Co Down, showing its three enclosures.

The visitor at the car-park is faced by a hillside with a series of substantial stone walls running along the slope. In plan these walls form three roughly oval concentric enclosures and they defined three distinct areas of the monastery. If you climb to the top of the ridge you will find the most important buildings in the inner enclosure: the church, round tower, graveyard and originally probably the abbot's house. The church is reduced to low foundations except for the west wall and door which were restored after excavation in the 1920s. The eastern part of the church and a small annexe to the north are later than the western end, dating from the Middle Ages. Reconstructed at the south-west corner of the church is an Early Christian period sundial, one of only three surviving in Ulster. The three main rays mark the times of the main daily services, at 9.00, 12 noon and 3.00. The area west of the church was the early graveyard and some stone graves are visible, while north-west of the church is the stump of a round tower. Now about 5 m high, it is partly reconstructed, perhaps of 10th-century date but difficult to date closely. To see a complete round tower in the north you have to go to Antrim or Devenish.

In the middle enclosure on the west side is a series of low foundations close to the wall which here forms a revetment and is not free-standing. The 1920s excavation suggested that the rectangular building was the monastic school or workshop, while the circular hut platforms nearby were craftworkshops. Elsewhere in the middle enclosure, but not now visible, would have been the kitchen and refectory and houses for the monks. Only part of the outer enclosure is accessible to the public. Its main feature, on the north side, is a circular kiln, very like corn-drying kilns found by excavation elsewhere to date from the 14th century. At the time of the early monastery there would have been gardens, orchards, pastures, barns and byres in the outer enclosure, as well as a 'porter's lodge' and a guesthouse for travellers.

These impressive remains on the ridge at Nendrum survive from a history of perhaps a thousand years of

Fig. 56 Nendrum: sundial and round tower stump.

activity. Mahee Island takes its name from St Mochaoi who died in the 490s and according to later tradition was converted to Christianity by St Patrick. He may have been an early missionary bishop in this area, but nothing certain is known about him. It is not until the 7th century that written sources begin to list churchmen associated with Nendrum, and the earliest finds from excavation are no earlier than the 7th century. Viking fleets were active in Strangford Lough, and the annals record that the erenagh (monastic official) was burned in his house in 976 and it is tempting to imagine a Viking raid.

It is unlikely that this event marked the end of life at Nendrum. John de Courcy (see *Feature 10*) who was active in founding new religious houses following his conquest of east Ulster chose Nendrum as the site for a small Benedictine monastery, linked with St Bee's Benedictine monastery on the Cumbrian coast (associated with an Irish female saint). The eastern extension of the church is thought to date from the Benedictine use of the site, and there is a burial ground on the east side of

the church from this medieval period. The Benedictine monastery seems to have been small; it is recorded that only two monks remained in 1288, and by the time of the papal taxation in 1302-6 Nendrum was listed as a parish church. The corn-drying kiln fits into this phase, for the rector of a parish church gathered in tithes of produce from his parishioners and would have needed a means to dry the corn. By the 15th or early 16th century, however, the island site had clearly become inconvenient and a new parish church was built at Tullynakill on the mainland nearby. Unlike Devenish, where burial continued, Nendrum seems to have been completely abandoned and it was forgotten, after perhaps a thousand years of ecclesiastical occupation.

The site was only rediscovered in the last century by Rev William Reeves (later Bishop of Down and Connor) during his research on the churches listed in the 1302-6 papal taxation. In 1844 he was staying in Comber, searching for the unknown church of *Nedrum*. He was directed to what the 1843 Ordnance Survey map marked as an 'old town' and shown what local people thought was a lime-kiln, but Reeves recognised it as the stump of a round tower. Reeves published his discovery but it was not until 1922-4 that the site was excavated, by Henry Lawlor and the Belfast Natural History and Philosophical Society. Unfortunately his excavation and restoration were poorly recorded and this has not helped our understanding of the complex development of the site. The stone structures which Lawlor identified and consolidated probably date from the later centuries of the Early Christian period (9th century onwards), and must have been preceded by generations of wooden buildings, of wattle, planks, thatch and wooden shingles.

Lawlor's excavation produced many finds but the one that has attracted most attention is the bell found near the outer wall on the north side. It is the common type of early ecclesiastical bell, of iron coated with bronze. Bells had practical uses, including marking the hours of

services, but with croziers they were also symbols of the authority of an abbot or bishop. There is a modern replica and a display of graveslabs and other carved stones in the small visitor centre on the site.

The lack of continuity in the occupation of Nendrum after the late medieval move to Tullynakill has proved important to archaeologists. So many early Irish monasteries have continued in use until modern times for burial that it is unusual to find one, like Nendrum, with no post-medieval disturbance. Despite the problems caused by Lawlor's excavations, Nendrum in its beautiful island setting provides the best example in Northern Ireland of the appearance of an Early Christian period monastery.

Lawlor, H C, *The monastery of St Mochaoi of Nendrum* (Belfast, 1925), to be used with caution; *An archaeological survey of Co Down* (HMSO, Belfast, 1966), 292-5; *Nendrum* (Belfast, 1986), DOE NI guidecard; a children's novel, *The bell of Nendrum*, by J S Andrews has been reprinted by Blackstaff Press (Belfast, 1985).

| 13. ARDBOE | High Cross, church and graveyard | Co Tyrone | H 966756 |

8 km ESE of Coagh, reached by turning S off the B73.

The site of Ardboe - *Ard Bó* ('height of the cow[s]') - is set on the west shore of Lough Neagh on a raised area of land with steep slopes to the east and south. The church here was founded by St Colmán mac Aed, probably in the 6th century. Little is known about its early history, but it was probably the site of a monastery, and in 1103 the death of a scholar of Ardboe is recorded in the annals - 'master of learning, liberality and poetry'. Ardboe was burned in 1166, and any early wooden buildings must have been destroyed.

The one link with the early monastery which does survive is a dramatic one - the fine high cross which greets the visitor on arrival. Though the sandstone is heavily weathered and the head of the cross is damaged, it is nevertheless the finest cross of the Early Christian period in Northern Ireland. On the east side (facing the graveyard) are Old Testament scenes, from the base Adam and Eve, the Sacrifice of Isaac, Daniel between lions and the Children in the Fiery Furnace. On the ringed head are a scene with an ecclesiastic holding a bell and crozier,

scales over flames, and Christ in Glory. The west side carries a series of New Testament scenes, from the Visit of the Magi at the base to the Crucifixion in the centre of the head. The panels on the narrow north and south sides are rather more varied, but they include Cain and Abel, David with the lion, David and Goliath, and the early desert fathers, Paul and Antony, receiving bread from a raven in the Egyptian desert (south) and the Slaughter of the Innocents and the Baptism (north).

Crosses in the Early Christian period served many purposes and could be 'read' on many different levels. They were a focus for prayer, preaching or penance, markers of special events or particular parts of the monastery, and 'sermons in stone'. With carved panels which were probably painted, the cross was a vivid 'visual aid' for an unlearned viewer, a reminder of the Bible story, from the Fall, through the Crucifixion, to Judgement and Salvation. To a member of the religious community it was a reminder of the eucharist, of the seasons of the church's year, and of the psalter (through

Fig. 57 West face of Ardboe Cross, Co Tyrone.

Fig. 58 Ardboe Cross: Daniel between the lions, on east face.

David, the psalmist/musician). The learned scholar could read yet more from the scenes. They point to prayers and litanies, and even to the importance of Sunday observance. This cross at Ardboe, dating probably from the 10th century, indicates a background of skilled craftsmanship and sophisticated scholarship in the late Early Christian period.

High crosses are one of the glories of Early Christian Ireland. A recent study has suggested a total of about 270 crosses for the whole of Ireland, embracing both decorated and plain examples. Many are incomplete or, like Ardboe, damaged and weathered, and the future safety and protection of these precious objects is a subject under active discussion. Moving a cross to an agreed indoor location and replacing it with a cast is one possible solution. Another is to build a shelter around and over the cross, but no course of action is without its problems and local acceptance would always be important.

In the large field north of the graveyard are two very badly ruined stone buildings, known as the 'abbey' and the 'cellar'. They have no features which can be dated, but they may be connected with the continuing use of the site in the Middle Ages for parish worship. Ardboe is valued at two marks in the papal taxation of 1302-6 (a mark was 13s 4d: the equivalent of 66p in modern money). The ruined church in the graveyard was built in the 17th century for Protestant worship but was abandoned in the early 18th century for the present Church of Ireland site. To maintain a link with the old site pieces of the old church, including stone window tracery, were built into the new church.

Two other features in the graveyard are worthy of note. Near the north-west corner is a dead beech tree, its trunk full of coins. This is the latest in a succession of such trees, known as 'pin wells' or 'pin trees', from the practice of hammering pins (now coins) into the trunk. Each pin or coin represents a wish or a prayer for a cure, and if a coin is removed it will carry the sickness with it. The metal does, however, gradually kill the tree. There could be continuity here going back a very long way indeed. It is known that pre-Christian Celts on the Continent revered trees, springs and wells, and it is clear that in Early Christian Ireland particular trees and water-sources were regarded with reverence. Holy wells, often associated with cures, are an important feature of the Irish landscape (see Chapter 11: Struell Wells). Special trees are far less common, and this tradition at Ardboe is a fascinating one.

Another feature in the graveyard points to a very different use: involvement in warfare in the late 16th and early 17th centuries. Part of the burial area is very markedly raised, and its shape to the west shows distinctive 'angle bastion' outlines, characteristic features of artillery forts. We know from written sources and pictorial maps that in the last years of the 16th century Hugh O'Neill held the west shore of Lough Neagh, facing Sir Arthur Chichester of Carrickfergus who held the Antrim shore. When the English advanced into this area (see Tullaghoge in Chapter 7 and *Feature 13*) they built forts at Mountjoy and *Dromboe*, which can probably be identified with Ardboe. The commanding point which the church had chosen a thousand years earlier proved attractive to the military tacticians in the early 17th century.

So within the long history of the site at Ardboe are elements of continuity and of change. The burning of the old church site in 1166 must have caused a break in continuity, yet as was often the case, the old monastic site continued in use for parish worship in the Middle Ages. The Elizabethan wars and the Plantation of the late 16th and early 17th centuries clearly caused major physical and social disruption and for a period the old site was used for Protestant worship. Burial has continued to the present day and the cross has remained a focus for the local community. There is a description of a pilgrimage here in the early 18th century. When Ardboe people emigrated in the early years of this century it was common for them to take a small chip of stone from the cross, and it was this practice that led to the erection of the iron railings. It is the continuing tradition that a member of a local family serves as the 'cross reader', ready to explain the carvings on the cross to visitors, and coffins are carried three times around the cross on their last journey to the graveyard.

Other crosses with figure carvings can be seen at Donaghmore, Co Tyrone (H 768654), Tynan, Co Armagh (H 758428), Donaghmore (J 104349) and Downpatrick (J 483445), both in Co Down, and Boho (H 116461) and Galloon (H 390226), both in Co Fermanagh.

Bigger, F J, and Fennell, W J, 'Ardboe, Co Tyrone: its cross and churches', *Ulster J Archaeol* 4 (1897-8), 1-7; Roe, H M, 'The High Crosses of east Tyrone', *Seanchas Ardmhacha* 2.1 (1956), 79-89; Hayes-McCoy, G A, *Ulster and other Irish maps c.1600* (Dublin, 1964), 30 and pl XIX; Hamlin, A, 'Dignatio diei dominici: an element in the iconography of Irish crosses?', *Ireland in early medieval Europe* (Cambridge, 1982), ed Whitelock, D, McKitterick, R, and Dumville, D, 69-75; Bourke, C, and Fry, M, 'Outdoors or in? The future of Ireland's stone crosses', *Archaeology Ireland* 3.2 (1989), 68-71; Harbison, P, *The High Crosses of Ireland: an iconographical and photographic survey* (Bonn, 1992); Fry, M, and Martin, A, 'Preserving by copying', *Archaeology Ireland* 8.1 (1994), 13. The cross figures prominently in Polly Devlin's *All of us there* (1983) and *The far side of the lough* (1983).

Fig. 59 Pin tree in Ardboe graveyard.

Fig. 60 Coins hammered into Ardboe pin tree.

FEATURE 8 THE VIKINGS

In the later Early Christian period there was a significant influx of pagan Scandinavian sea pirates into Ireland resulting in major economic, social and political changes within society.

The Vikings arrived not as a single, unified political force, nor as part of a pre-planned invasion, but as small groups, usually of Norwegian origin, intent on making ecomonic gains for themselves through raiding. The activity of these raiders must be seen as a part of the general Scandinavian overseas expansion that occurred in the last centuries of the first millennium AD throughout northern Europe and, in particular, as an extension of their activity in the northern and western Isles of Scotland. In the first period of Viking action (AD 795-835) they were mainly concerned with small-scale, hit-and-run raids on churches and monasteries. Priceless objects of religious art in gold and silver were looted. The monasteries were also known to be centres of human population and the Vikings carried off captives to be sold as slaves. In the face of this threat there was no united military response, since Irish society was made up of numerous small kingdoms often quarrelling with one another.

In the second phase of Viking activity (AD 835-880) the sea pirates established a number of settlements in coastal areas, began to overwinter in Ireland and carried out raids inland. While this made them a more dangerous threat, it also meant that they had lost the advantage of seaborne escape after a raid, and they could be attacked in their camps by the Irish. In Ulster they suffered heavy defeat in AD 866 at the hands of Aedh Findliath ('Aedh the light grey') of the Cenél Eóghain (the Uí Néill high king) who plundered their settlements on the north coast. These settlements were probably fortified enclosures, protecting the harbours where their longships would be docked. At Cork, Dublin, Limerick and Waterford similar encampments were destined to develop into permanent trading settlements by the 10th century. In Ulster, however, no modern towns have been definitely shown to have had origins in the Viking Age. Larne, a town certainly in existence by the 12th century, may have begun as a Viking settlement, but there is no archaeological evidence yet to prove this. The third phase of Viking activity (AD 914-980) began a new wave of plundering, but the establishment of the 10th-century towns led to change. The Vikings who settled as traders were gradually assimilated into Irish society through inter-marriage with local inhabitants and the acceptance of Christianity. By the mid 10th century the settlers had become so integrated into the existing population that they can reasonably be called the Hiberno-Norse.

Physical evidence of the presence of Vikings in Ulster is very limited. No Viking encampments have yet been discovered, and our knowledge of their activity rests on documentary accounts, place-names, a few burials, and isolated hoards of coins and

Fig. 61 Hiberno-Norse weapons (9th – 10th-century) from the river Blackwater (Ulster Museum).

valuables. The documentary evidence consists mainly of the often terse entries recorded by monks in the annals. The first such entry is in the *Annals of Ulster* in the year AD 795 where it is recorded that the heathen burnt *Rechru*. This may refer to the island monastery of Lambay, Co Dublin, but it is also possible that *Rechru* was Rathlin Island, Co Antrim. If this was so, then this small, windswept island was the first recorded place in Ireland to suffer from Viking aggression. Further attacks followed quickly and the brief accounts given in the annals only hint at the social and economic disruption caused by the raids. The annals also record where the Vikings established their encampments. In the 9th century they were to be found in Lough Foyle, Lough Neagh, Lough Erne, Belfast Lough, Strangford Lough and Carlingford Lough. In the last two cases Viking place-names have survived to the present day. The names 'Carlingford' and 'Strangford' contain the Viking word *fjord*, which means a bay or sea-inlet. Indeed the modern province name 'Ulster' appears to be a Viking form, based on the Irish population name Ulaidh.

Since the Vikings were a pagan people they often deposited grave-goods with their dead for use in the afterlife. For the archaeologist this means that a grave containing such grave-goods can be identified as being that of a Viking since their Irish Christian contemporaries did not usually include objects of jewellery, coins or weapons with their dead. Unfortunately no Viking burials have been unearthed by archaeologists in Ulster in recent years, though at least four definite or probable burials discovered in previous centuries are recorded.

In 1784 possible Viking burials were discovered in an Early Bronze Age cemetery in Church Bay on Rathlin Island, one of which contained a body with a silver brooch of the 9th century with definite Viking stylistic features. Near Larne, Co Antrim, in 1840 workmen constructing a railway line along the coast came across a burial in the sand with Viking grave-goods, including an iron sword, an iron spear, a bone comb, and a bronze ringed pin, helping to date the grave to the late 9th or early 10th century. At Ballywillin Bog, Co Londonderry, a possible ship-burial was found in a peat bog in 1813. The vessel was well preserved by the peat (see *Feature 9*) and its oak timbers were carried away in several cart-loads. It was estimated that the boat could have transported 40 or 50 tons and it lay under a mound of stones, clay and peat. While it is not definite that this was a Viking ship-burial, the boat was certainly buried in a manner characteristic of a Viking period burial and this may have been the last resting-place for some Norse warrior who died during a raid in Ulster. Two brooches and a bronze bowl were found in a probable

Viking burial in the raised beach at Ballyholme Bay in Bangor, Co Down, in 1903. The few burials found in Ulster suggest that Viking settlement was limited. The Uí Néill successes against the Vikings in Ulster may have meant that they were never in a position to establish more permanent settlements, and this may explain why they are so poorly represented in the archaeological record of the north.

Fig. 62 Hiberno-Norse silver (9th – 10th-century) from the river Blackwater (Ulster Museum).

The discovery of hoards of silver, gold and coins provides further evidence of a Viking presence in Ulster. These hoards are groups of valuable objects or coins that were deposited in the ground for safe keeping. There are 120 examples of Viking Age hoards known from the whole of Ireland, the majority deposited in the years between AD 920 and 1000. This period coincided with the growth of the Viking trade centres such as Dublin or Wexford, but it was also a time of increased violence within society. In Ulster hoards are recorded in coastal areas and in and around Armagh City, including groups from Ballycastle and Derrykeighan, both in Co Antrim, and Scrabo Hill, Co Down. The Vikings introduced silver bullion and coinage into Ireland through their trade networks. By the

9th century the Irish had adopted silver for use in their financial dealings and by the 10th century Viking-derived coins were being used. The coins and bullion found in hoards may be Viking payment to Irish chiefs for slaves or other 'commodities'.

While the evidence for the presence of Vikings in Ulster is limited, it would be wrong to imagine that the north did not benefit from the positive contributions which the Scandinavians made to Ireland, especially in that later period when they had settled down as traders. The raiding, destruction, violence and slave trading of the earlier years of Viking activity should not be forgotten, but nor should their contributions to Irish society. New sophisticated techniques in smithing and new weapons like the long sword were readily adopted by the Irish. Superior Viking ship technology led to improvements in sea travel. Coins were introduced into the economy and the Viking trading ports opened Ireland up to the trade routes of Europe and the Near East.

Milligan, S F, 'Danish finds in Ireland', *JRSAI* 36 (1906), 205-6; Fanning, T, 'The Viking gravegoods discovered near Larne, Co Antrim in 1840', *JRSAI* 100 (1970), 71-8; Hall, R, 'A checklist of Viking Age coin finds from Ireland', *Ulster J Archaeol* 36 & 37 (1973-74), 71-86; Warner, R, 'The reprovenancing of two important penannular brooches of the Viking period', *Ulster J Archaeol* 36 & 37 (1973-74), 58-70; Briggs, C S, 'A boat-burial from Co Antrim', *Medieval Archaeology* 18 (1974), 158-60; Flanagan, M, 'The Vikings', *The people of Ireland* (Belfast, 1988), ed Loughrey, P, 55-84; Mallory, J P, and McNeill, T E, *The archaeology of Ulster* (Belfast, 1991), 226-37; Roesdahl, E, *The Vikings* (London, 1991). Issue 9.3 (1995) of *Archaeology Ireland* contains a variety of articles on the Vikings in Ireland.

Fig. 63 Rough Fort, Risk, Co Down (Infra-red photograph by Tony Corey).

Chapter 7

Early Christian Settlement in the Landscape

0.5 km W of Moira village, in a bend on the Old Kilmore Road.

Rough Fort is a small, well-preserved rath set on the outskirts of Moira. It has a raised central area surrounded by a deep ditch and a single earthen bank. An outer ditch is also visible, though now largely silted up. A causeway on the east side provides access to the central area. It is difficult to imagine that this earthwork was once a busy defended settlement of the Early Christian period, and the home of farmers who practised mixed agriculture and craftworking.

With a total of somewhere between 30,000 and 40,000 examples, raths (or ring-forts) are the most common ancient monument in Ireland. Only about 200 have been excavated, however, which restricts our understanding of raths to the information gathered from a limited number of sites. Over 50 have been excavated in Northern Ireland and the evidence suggests that they became the characteristic settlement type in the landscape during the 6th to 7th centuries AD. At present there is no evidence to suggest that raths continued to be built after the coming of the Anglo-Normans to Ireland, nor that raths were lived in after the 13th century, though some were reused in later warfare.

Rough Fort is a rath with a single bank – a type sometimes called 'univallate'. The earthen bank was thrown up using the soil dug from the ditch. A timber palisade was built on top of the bank to give added defence against raids. Some raths may have two, three or even four circles of banks and ditches surrounding the internal area. These 'multivallate' sites were probably high status habitations, homes of Early Christian period kings. The location of the entrance on the east side of the perimeter of Rough Fort is a feature common at other raths.

The inner area enclosed by the earthworks probably contained post-and-wattle farmhouses and outhouses. Our understanding of the techniques used in building these structures was greatly increased by the excavation of waterlogged levels in a rath at Deer Park Farms, Co Antrim (see *Feature 9*). Excavation has produced evidence that a change from round to rectangular houses was taking place in eastern Ulster in the 8th and 9th centuries AD. Since Rough Fort has never been excavated we do not know its date of construction or what kind of houses its occupants built. A structure found at many raths is the souterrain, but only excavation or geophysical

Fig. 64 Rough Fort, Risk, Co Down: view across banks.

In the Early Christian period a rath would have formed part of a farming landscape of field-systems and enclosures. In the constant reorganisation of the countryside which has taken place over the intervening centuries the old field divisions have been replaced or abandoned. It is now only in upland areas like Ballyutoag (J 274796), Co Antrim, that research can identify the remains of these features as faint traces in the landscape. Rough Fort remained an isolated monument surrounded by later field boundaries until the early 1970s, when the suburbs of Moira began to grow in this direction and its owner placed it in State Care. The result is that the 1,000-year-old farmstead now stands in the middle of 20th-century housing.

Fig. 65 Reconstruction drawing of a rath.

In the folklore of the countryside raths were known as 'Danes forts' or 'fairy forts' and beliefs and stories often grew up around them. These beliefs are now dying out, and with them has faded the belief in retribution from the fairy spirits for any damage done to their homes. Though they were once so numerous, many raths have been destroyed in recent times and they are still in danger from agricultural improvement schemes or construction works. However, raths represent the tangible evidence of a 1,000-year-old landscape and, like Rough Fort, they deserve to be preserved and cherished.

prospecting could reveal if a souterrain was present at this site (see this chapter: Drumena cashel and souterrain). The raised central area at Rough Fort may have been formed by depositing ditch spoil to produce a platform on which to build houses. This has been found to have been the case by excavation at a number of sites, where the ditch spoil was used to construct a low platform 1 m or less in height, but prolonged occupation or deliberate heightening of the internal area of a rath could produce a central mound up to 4 m high. The rath at Deer Park Farms was an example of such a 'raised rath', but without excavation raised raths can sometimes be difficult to distinguish from the later earthen castles of the Anglo-Norman period (see Chapter 8: Duneight).

Other small 'univallate' raths similar to Rough Fort are found throughout Northern Ireland. To check if there are any examples in your own area you should consult the 1:50,000 and 1:10,000 Ordnance Survey map series. Lisnagade (J 086440) and Lisnavaragh (J 081442) are fine examples of 'multivallate' raths near Scarva in Co Down.

Lynn, C J, 'Some 'early' ring-forts and crannogs', *Journal of Irish Archaeology* 1 (1983), 47-58; Williams, B B, 'Early Christian landscapes in County Antrim', *Landscape archaeology in Ireland*, British Archaeological Report 116 (1983), ed Reeves-Smyth, T, and Hamond, F, 233-46; Williams, B B, 'Excavations at Ballyutoag, Co Antrim', *Ulster J Archaeol* 47 (1984), 37-49; Edwards, N, *The archaeology of early medieval Ireland* (London, 1990), 6-33.

Raths

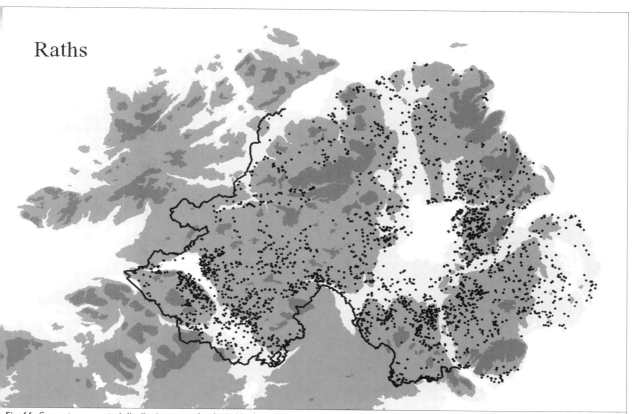

Fig. 66 Computer-generated distribution map of raths in Northern Ireland (Michael Avery).

Fig. 67 Rough Fort: aerial view showing the rath surrounded by modern housing.

15. DRUMENA   Cashel and souterrain   Co Down   J 312340

3.6 km SW of Castlewellan, approached from a minor road ESE off the A25 road to Rathfriland, east of Lough Island Reavy reservoir.

Fig. 68 Drumena Cashel, Co Down, before restoration in the early 20th century, Green Collection, WAG 1434 (Ulster Folk & Transport Museum).

This simple drystone-walled enclosure is situated on the northern slopes of the stoney ridge of Drumena, in the northern foothills of the Mourne Mountains. The monument – a cashel – is approached by a path which brings the visitor to a narrow opening on its north side. The enclosure is oval in plan with a larger entrance on the east side. The internal area may seem to have few obvious archaeological features except some uneven, stoney patches and a small souterrain. This is T-shaped in plan and can be entered down a flight of steps at the north-east end which leads into a passageway. The roof of the souterrain passage is made of large stone slabs, but modern concrete lintels can also be seen. At the end of this passage is a second entrance to the south-east, directly opposite a small rectangular chamber.

Fig. 69 Drumena Cashel.

Fig. 70 Reconstruction drawing of a souterrain, showing underground passageway leading from house.

Known locally as Walsh's Fort, this cashel survived because of the interest of the Belfast Natural History and Philosophical Society in the 1920s. The monument was in danger of being destroyed by a road contractor, but the Society paid the princely sum of £150 in 1925-6 to excavate and restore the ruin. When they started their work the site looked very different from how it appears today. The drystone wall had collapsed and the inner area was heavily overgrown. The fallen stones were cleared away from the inner base of the cashel wall until the original wall face and foundations were exposed. The fallen stones were then relaid on the foundations and the wall was rebuilt. The souterrain was cleared of debris and restored at the same time. Sections of the roof that had collapsed were replaced with concrete lintels.

The excavations established how the cashel wall (3.3 to 3.6 m thick) had been built. A bottom course of large boulders had been laid on the ground surface. On this two drystone walls were built and the space between was filled with small stones. Originally possibly 3 m high, the wall now stands to a height of about 2.75 m. The cashel was the stone-built equivalent of the Early Christian period rath and was the home of similar prosperous farming people. The difference is that the cashels were built in stony, hilly areas. The people adapted to their local environment, just as the crannog dwellers did (see this chapter: Lough na Cranagh), by using the

readily available supply of stone to build the walls of their enclosures.

The houses of the Early Christian farmers stood within the enclosure and the confused areas of stone may be the foundations of their homes. A number of hearths found during the excavations may mark the fireplaces of houses, or perhaps they were connected with industrial activities like metalworking. The entrance on the east may have been the original way into the cashel, or possibly it is a later opening made to allow carts into the interior when the site was reused as a farmyard in the recent past.

The souterrain is an artifical 'cave', an underground chamber and passage of a type also found at raths, monasteries and other Early Christian settlements. The original entrance to this souterrain was not at the north-east but at the south-east end. This opening leads into the T-shaped head of the souterrain, directly opposite a rectangular chamber. A small hole in the wall of this chamber may have been a ventilation gap. Recent research has recorded some 750 stone-built souterrains in Northern Ireland. Most souterrains are in a very dangerous condition and should not be entered for safety reasons. A souterrain could be constructed in a number of ways. A trench could be dug and its sides lined with drystone walls; a roof of large flat stones would be added and the entire structure covered with earth, leaving it hidden from view. Alternatively, the souterrain could be cut out of rock, but this was more laborious and is less commonly found. At Coolcran, Co Fermanagh, excavations in 1983 in a rath revealed a wooden souterrain, the first of its kind discovered in Ulster, which was dated to the 9th century using dendrochronology (see *Feature 7*).

The use of souterrains has long been debated. The dark passages with their twists, turns and narrow entrances into side chambers would suggest that they were used as refuges in times of danger. There was a flourishing slave trade during the Viking period (see *Feature 8*), and during an attack on a settlement the inhabitants could have escaped into the souterrain with their valuables. Any enemy who discovered the entrance and tried to investigate would be vulnerable to attack as they squeezed through one of the narrow entrances into a side chamber in the dark. It has also been suggested that souterrains could have been used as cellars in which food was stored because the temperature in them is very constant.

Cashels were abandoned as a settlement type by the 13th century and there is little archaeological evidence that occupation of cashels continued into the late medieval period. However, they must have remained useful as enclosures for stock and were certainly reused for such purposes. In stony areas, like the Glens of Antrim, the Mournes and parts of Co Fermanagh, stone enclosures very similar to cashels were being built and used into this century to keep stock secure. The response to the stony environment that was appropriate in the Early Christian period was still appropriate to a hill farmer in recent times.

Another example of a cashel can be seen at Altagore, Co Antrim (D 249349) and a rock-cut souterrain can be found to the north of the graveyard at Ballintemple, Co Londonderry (C 810149).

Berry, Colonel R G, 'Report on the work carried out at Drumena', *Proceeedings of the Belfast Natural History and Philosophical Society* (1926-27), 46-55; Warner, R, 'The Irish souterrains and their background', *Subterranean Britain* (London, 1979), ed Crawford, H, 100-44; Williams, B B, 'Excavation of a rath at Coolcran, County Fermanagh', *Ulster J Archaeol* 48 (1985), 69-80; Edwards, N, *The archaeology of early medieval Ireland* (London, 1990), 6-33.

16. LOUGH NA CRANAGH | Crannog Co Antrim | D 178427

Lough na Cranagh is one of two loughs in depressions on the top of Fair Head, 6.4 km ENE of Ballycastle. The crannog can be viewed from the lough-shore.

The visitor to Fair Head will see a small 'island' in the middle of Lough na Cranagh. This is not a natural island but is an artificial structure called a crannog. The crannog here is oval, with a drystone-wall revetment which rises about 1.5 m above the water-level of the lough. The wall is double-faced, with the space between filled with a rubble core. The site was excavated in 1888 but the techniques used were of a poor standard. Extensive excavation produced a few stone artifacts and animal bones, but no date was suggested for the construction or occupation of the site. The excavation did show that the crannog was built of large blocks of basalt, well fitted together without mortar. The surface of the crannog was covered with stone slabs and at the centre of this floor was a layer of charred sand several centimetres thick, perhaps the remains of a hearth.

Excavations at crannog sites have produced evidence of settlement ranging from the Mesolithic to the late medieval period. It is now thought likely that activity dating from the Late Bronze Age and earlier is related to hunting and fishing settlements. Late Bronze Age lake dwellings tend to be restricted to small-scale building activity on natural islands. Oak timbers removed from the foundations of six Ulster crannogs have supplied dendrochronological dates (see *Feature 7*) for construction clustering in the period AD 550 to 620. These Early Christian period crannogs are in strong contrast to earlier, prehistoric lake dwellings. Either founded on natural islands or totally artificial, they all show a heavy investment of work and resources into producing substantial and defensive platforms. The crannog is seen primarily as an Early

Fig. 71 Aerial view of Fair Head, Co Antrim, with crannog visible in the centre of Lough na Cranagh.

Christian period type, the wetland equivalent to and contemporary of raths and cashels.

A ring of timber piles was driven vertically into the lake-bed to provide firm foundations and a stout enclosing framework which would protect the structure from wave erosion. If the timber piles were carried up beyond the surface of the water they would also provide the island with a palisade or fence which could be used to protect and defend the site from attack. Into this framework, a mixture of brushwood, stones, clay and debris was piled to raise the level and create a surface for buildings. At Lough na Cranagh the perimeter of the crannog was of a more solid nature since it was constructed with stone blocks. It was founded on a submerged rock outcrop and a damaged section of the wall on the north-west side reveals that the platform was constructed on layers of boulders. The extensive use of stone at this lake settlement may reflect a scarcity of timber resources available to the Early Christian builders living in the craggy landscape of Fair Head.

A figure of 1,200 crannogs has been suggested for the whole of Ireland. Within Northern Ireland crannogs are found in all areas with shallow lakes, but there is a particular concentration of sites in areas of extensive lakeland like Co Fermanagh. It was once thought that the crannog was a settlement type restricted to Ireland and Scotland, but recent research has identified an example dating from the 10th century at Llangorse Lake in south Wales.

Crannogs are most easily recognised as small 'islands' in lakes, often with a cluster of trees and bushes. Others appear as slight mounds in areas which were once loughs but which have been partly or totally drained for land reclamation. The wetland location of crannogs is important to archaeology since these waterlogged conditions lead to excellent preservation of organic materials like wood, leather and bone (see *Features 9* and *14*), materials which would usually have perished on dryland settlement sites like raths. These organic remains can tell us a great

Fig. 72 Lough na Cranagh: the crannog's stone wall.

deal about how the people lived on these structures – their everyday tools and weapons, their diet, their crafts and how they built the crannog itself.

The deliberate building of crannogs in watery locations with restricted access indicates their defensive nature. Crannogs could be approached in dug-out boats, and at Lough na Cranagh the crannog has three possible landing bays. Two lines of boulders lie under the water next an indent in the north face of the oval perimeter wall. The boulder lines may have formed the arms of a small harbour. A second indent, on the south-east side of the perimeter wall, perhaps marks the location of a sheltered mooring. A group of boulders extending from the crannog below the water surface at this point may have been part of an associated jetty. Finally, a flight of crude stone steps on the north-west leads down to an underwater ridge of bedrock extending towards the lough shore and some form of jetty may once have stood on the ridge.

As Chris Lynn has pointed out, safety from surprise attack seems to have been of more importance to their inhabitants than ready access to land. Many artefacts of a rich and luxurious nature have been found on crannog sites, including fine metalwork and imported pottery, some of Mediterranean origin, which suggests that these were the habitations of the highest ranking members of Early Christian society. Lagore Crannog, Co Meath, has been identified with the Uí Néill royal site of *Loch Gabhair*. Evidence of fine metalworking and industrial activity at Moynagh, Co Meath, suggests that this crannog was home for a wealthy, skilled metalworker. Richard Warner believes that the crannog was used as a defended dwelling by those of high status and wealth as a means of security, akin to the souterrain in the settlements of people of lower status. While Moynagh showed clear evidence of settlement occupation, other crannog sites (such as Lisleitrim, Co Armagh) are located close to major multivallate raths, and these crannogs may have been 'bolt-holes' where those of wealth and status could shelter in times of danger. It is

Fig. 73 Richard Bartlett's drawing of a crannog under attack (National Library of Ireland).

possible that the crannog at Lough na Cranagh may have been a refuge for the occupants of the nearby settlement of Doonmore (D 172426), clear as a prominent mound on the horizon 700 m to the west. Gordon Childe excavated this site in the 1930s. He thought it was a Norman motte and bailey castle, but only a few of the finds he recovered were obviously Norman. Souterrain Ware pottery was scattered all over the site and he admitted that most of his finds were more in keeping with those to be found at a cashel or souterrain. While there may have been some Norman use of the site at a later date, Doonmore has certain similarities with excavated Early Christian period forts in south-west Scotland.

The defensive qualities of crannogs meant that they were sometimes reused in late medieval times and even later. Several well-known pictorial maps by Richard Bartlett from around AD 1600-1602 show a crannog under attack in Co Tyrone. If a crannog was near to a fortified site on shore a lord could use it as a refuge in times of danger, just as his ancestors had done long before. In addition, crannogs were used as secure locations where hostages could be kept. In recent times the inaccessible nature of the crannog has made it a favoured haunt for those engaged in the illicit distilling of whiskey.

Other crannogs can be seen from the road in Lough Brickland, Co Down (J 111412), Roughan Lough (H 828687) and Carnteel Lough (H 695546), both in Co Tyrone, and many places in Co Fermanagh.

McHenry, A, 'Lough na Cranagh', *PRIA*, Section C, 2 (1879-88), 462; Childe, V G, 'Doonmore, a castle mound near Fair Head', *Ulster J Archaeol* 1 (1938), 122-35; Lynn, C J, 'Some 'early' ringforts and crannogs', *Journal of Irish Archaeology* 1 (1983), 47-58; Campbell, E, and Lane, A, 'Llangorse: a tenth century royal crannog in Wales', *Antiquity* 63 (1989), 675-81; Edwards, N, *The archaeology of early medieval Ireland* (London, 1990), 34-41; Warner, R, 'On crannogs and kings: Part 1', *Ulster J Archaeology* 57 (1994), 61-9; Bradley, J, 'Living at the water's edge', *Archaeology Ireland* 10.1 (1996), 24-6.

17. TULLAGHOGE | Hilltop enclosure   Co Tyrone | H 825743

On the crown of a prominent hill, 4 km SSE of Cookstown, east of the B162 and near the village of Tullyhogue. Car-park at the foot of the hill.

Fig. 74 Tullaghoge, Co Tyrone: aerial view.

The outer bank of this monument is planted with mature trees, making it a prominent feature of the landscape, visible from far away. From the small car-park the visitor is invited to walk up a steep concrete lane to reach the site. This uphill climb is rewarded with magnificent views of the countryside in all directions, even on the most overcast of days.

The visitor enters the circular earthwork through a gap in the outer bank, one of two banks which encircle the monument. The two high banks are set wide apart with a flat area between them, but there is no outer ditch. A causeway leads to a gap in the inner bank, giving access to the inner enclosed area.

The first impression may be that this monument looks very like an Early Christian period bivallate rath (see this chapter: Rough Fort, Risk) but any such impression is superficial. The unusual ground plan of this earthwork distinguishes it from the main body of bivallate raths in Ulster. Tullaghoge does not have any defensive outer ditch, and its banks are not set closely together. A bivallate rath has two concentric rings of banks and ditches designed for defensive strength. The difference is probably explained by the fact that Tullaghoge was a royal power centre and not a defended farmstead. The earthworks here defined an area of ritual importance; they did not protect the site from attack.

Fig. 75 Tullaghoge: outer and inner banks of enclosure.

Tullaghoge ('mound of the young men/warriors') emerges into history in the 11th century when it was the dynastic centre and inauguration place for the Cenél Eóghain (later to be called the northern O'Neills). On the hillslope outside the enclosure stood the *Leac na Rí* - the Stone of the Kings - where the coronation or 'making' of the new O'Neill king took place. It is likely, however, that Tullaghoge had some ritual importance before the O'Neill expansion south-east over the Sperrins in the 11th century, although we do not know the date when the earthwork was built. The enclosure and the land surrounding Tullaghoge was under the hereditary control of one of the principal supporting families of the O'Neills, the O'Hagans - the old Irish name for the area being Ballyhagan. Their traditional burial ground was the circular walled graveyard of Donaghrisk, a quarter of a mile south-west of the enclosure. This family, and the O'Cahans or O'Kanes, played an important part in the inauguration ceremony of an O'Neill king (see Chapter 10: Dungiven Priory, and also *Feature 13*).

The last of the O'Neills to be inaugurated at Tullaghoge was probably Hugh O'Neill in 1595. In September 1602 Lord Mountjoy underlined his significant victory at Kinsale, Co Cork, in the previous year with four or five days of destruction of the heartland of O'Neill territory in south-east Tyrone. Tullaghoge was especially targeted by Mountjoy, and the 'Stone of the Kings' was smashed to pieces in a telling gesture to emphasise the end of O'Neill kingship in Ulster. After the destruction of the chair some fragments were supposedly still to be found in the area in 1768, although there was a tradition that the last known fragment was built into a coach-house in the early 18th century.

We are very fortunate to have two surviving pictorial maps of this area. The first, by Richard Bartlett and dated to about 1601, shows Tullaghoge with the inauguration chair on the hillslope. The enclosure has two gateways and there are two thatched houses in the inner area. One is a small house, and the other is a larger, two-storey building.

Fig. 76 Richard Bartlett's drawing of the *Leac na Rí* and Tullaghoge enclosure (National Library of Ireland).

The chair seems to consist of a large boulder with three stone slabs surrounding it, forming a throne-like structure. In the second pictorial map, of a similar date and possibly also the work of Bartlett, the coronation ceremony is shown. Seven individuals are grouped around the O'Neill, seated in the chair. One person on the right, probably O'Hagan, holds what appears to be a shoe over the head of O'Neill, while a second figure, on the left and probably O'Cahan, holds the side of the chair. The other five members of the group are probably the leaders of the other main clans. The shoe is probably to show that the new king would walk worthily in the footsteps of his predecessors.

At the time of the Plantation (see *Feature 13*), a grant of 1610 records Robert Lindsey as the new owner of 1000 acres surrounding Tullaghoge. He must have died soon after, for by the time of Pynnar's Survey of 1619 the land is owned by his widow, who was living in the enclosure, using its banks as a bawn and residing with her family in a timber house. By 1622, however, another survey records that the family had abandoned this house and the enclosure was completely deserted. Mrs Lindsey had moved to a thatched house at the foot of the hill. But the former importance of Tullaghoge was certainly not forgotten. Local people, historians, and antiquarians continued to regard the site with great esteem. The tradition has continued into this century and one of the monument's recent benefactors was Mr J Tullyhogue O'Hagan.

Other probable inauguration sites are Cornashee, near Lisnakea, Co Fermanagh (H 367348) and Navan Fort, Co Armagh (H 847452). The inauguration chair of the Clandeboy O'Neills can be seen in the Ulster Museum, Belfast.

Hore, H P, 'Inauguration of Irish chiefs', *Ulster J Archaeol* 5 (1857), 216-24; Treadwell, V, 'The survey of Armagh and Tyrone', *Ulster J Archaeol* 27 (1964), 140-54; Hayes-McCoy, G A, 'The making of an O'Neill: a view of the ceremony at Tullaghoge, Co Tyrone', *Ulster J Archaeol* 33 (1970), 89-94.

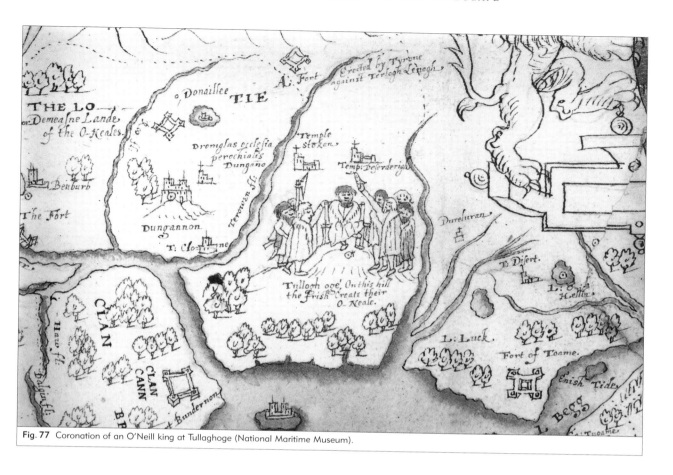

Fig. 77 Coronation of an O'Neill king at Tullaghoge (National Maritime Museum).

FEATURE 9 | WETLAND PRESERVATION IN ARCHAEOLOGY

Fig. 78 Deer Park Farms, Co Antrim: oak door-jambs from entrance of wicker house.

Throughout the past our ancestors made much use of organic materials in their daily lives. Materials like wood, straw, textiles, and leather were used for house building, making clothes and manufacturing tools. On excavations at dryland sites the survival of organic materials is usually poor, but on wetland sites there is a much greater chance of organic materials surviving. This is because the remains are protected from decay by silts, mud or peat which seal them in a wet, airless environment, free from the bacteria and fungi which would destroy them in dry conditions.

About one-seventh of the land surface of Ireland is covered by peat bogs providing wet conditions ideal for the preservation of lost or buried artefacts and structures. Since 1750 over 96 examples of 'bog bodies' have been discovered in Ireland. Unlike the famous north-west European bog bodies (like Tollund Man), most of which date from the Iron Age, or Lindow Man in England, who died in the Iron Age, the majority of Irish bodies are of

late medieval or modern date, although a number of examples have been dated by radiocarbon (see *Feature 2*) to prehistoric times.

Between 1985 and 1989 Barry Raftery carried out investigations in Co Longford and Co Galway on a series of wooden tracks buried in the peat. The tracks had been laid down across bogs from prehistoric to Early Christian times, to allow safe passage for travellers journeying across the dangerous terrain. Peat later grew over the trackways and covered them, but this meant that they were preserved

Fig. 79 Deer Park Farms: wooden shoe-last discovered during excavation.

from decay. Fifty-seven wooden track-ways were uncovered, and doubtless many more still lie hidden in peat bogs throughout Ireland.

Waterlogging at dryland sites can also lead to the preservation of organic remains. Excavations in the old waterfronts of towns have often yielded waterlogged remains. In Dublin the waterlogged foundations of over 200 10th- to 11th-century wooden buildings have been excavated. In Northern Ireland the waterlogging of the lower levels of a raised rath at Deer Park Farms, near Carnlough, Co Antrim, helped to preserve unique information about this Early Christian homestead. The site had been occupied between about AD 600 and 1000, but at some time around AD 750 the inhabitants decided to heighten the damp, midden-filled interior of their settlement. All the old buildings were demolished or pushed over and covered with earth. Impeded drainage and the damp, buried midden produced waterlogging in the lower levels of the rath. In one

area archaeologists came across a deposit of preserved organic material 1.5 m deep and within this the hazel wickerwork walls of several houses had been perfectly preserved. It was possible to see exactly how the walls of the circular wicker houses had been constructed in Early Christian times. Organic artifacts which had been preserved included wooden vessels, scraps of textile, parts of leather shoes and a wooden shoe-last.

Less obvious but no less valuable archaeological evidence can also be preserved on wetland sites. Pollen grains (see *Feature 5*) and remains of plants allow us to reconstruct the surrounding environment, while insects and parasite eggs tell us about the conditions of life in an ancient settlement. The study of tool-marks on wooden artifacts and structures can reveal the carpentry skills of past centuries, as on the central oak post of the Navan multi-ring structure (see Chapter 5).

While it is clear that wetland archaeology can greatly increase our

knowledge of the past there is a major problem. As soon as preserved organic materials are exposed to the air they begin to deteriorate and decay. Wooden objects will dry and crack almost at once. Organic remains must therefore be kept in a wet condition on site until they can be taken to a laboratory for chemical treatment or freeze-drying. Laboratory processes are expensive and it has been estimated that a wetland excavation can cost up to four times as much as a dryland excavation, but clearly both are needed for our knowledge to advance.

Coles, J, *The archaeology of wetlands* (Edinburgh, 1984); Ó Floinn, R, 'Irish bog bodies', *Archaeology Ireland* 2.3 (1988), 94-7; Lynn, C, 'Deer Park Farms', *Current Archaeology* 113 (1989), 193-8; Raftery, B, *Trackways through time* (Dublin, 1990); Renfrew, C, and Bahn, P, *Archaeology: theories, methods and practice* (London, 1991), 58-60; Ó Floinn, R, 'Recent research into Irish bog bodies' and 'Gazetteer of bog bodies in Ireland', *Bog bodies: new discoveries and new perspectives* (London, 1995), ed Turner, R C, and Scaife, R G, 137-45 and 221-34.

Fig. 80 Dundrum Castle, Co Down (Infra-red photograph by Tony Corey).

Chapter 8
The Anglo-Normans

In Carrickfergus town, 16 km NE of Belfast on the A2 coast road to Larne.

Carrickfergus Castle is the best known, and certainly the best preserved, Anglo-Norman castle in Northern Ireland. For more than 800 years it has stood watch over the northern shore of Belfast Lough, providing protection for the historic town that grew up in its shadow. While other Anglo-Norman castles were abandoned, Carrickfergus Castle maintained its strategic importance as a military stronghold on the east coast of Ulster, remaining the centre of English administration in the Earldom throughout the later medieval period. From Tudor times onwards it was adapted for defence with guns and cannon. It continued in military use until it was placed in State Care as an ancient monument in 1928.

Visitors arriving at the castle should begin their tour at the keep on the southern tip of the rocky promontory, furthest from the gatehouse. The keep and the courtyard in which it stands belong to the earliest phase in the castle's history. Work began on the building of this inner ward and the strong rectangular keep soon after John de Courcy's arrival in Ulster in 1177 (see *Feature 10*). This was his principal castle and he recognised the defensive strength of the rocky promontory which jutted out into

the sea. From Carrickfergus he was able to guard against any intrusion into his territory by sea while remaining in close contact with his allies across the Irish Sea. The building of a stone castle involved a huge expenditure of time and resources but de Courcy needed a strong stone castle to keep his host of enemies at bay in the early years of his lordship in Ulster. There was also a symbolic value in its construction: it confirmed to his Irish neighbours his new position of power and the intended permanent nature of that power.

The stone keep has four main storeys, and is entered on the first floor by an outside stair. Access between floors was by a narrow spiral stone stair rising through the full height in the wall thickness at the south-east corner. The keep seems to have been designed mainly for the function of providing the new lord and his family with secure, private accommodation. A hall in the inner ward was used for the public life of the castle. This was the time when kings and great magnates were gradually withdrawing from the communal lifestyle of previous centuries. Their grandfathers may have shared their homes with soldiers and retainers but there was now a trend for lords to

Fig. 81 Carrickfergus Castle, Co Antrim.

distance themselves from the extended household. The accommodation that John de Courcy provided for himself in the keep was truly fit for a king. Indeed, King John spent ten days at the castle in July 1210.

The visitor moves from this inner ward to a middle ward through a 19th-century gateway. The early castle had proved to be ill defended on its east side. To correct this weakness the middle ward was added at some time during the years 1216 to 1222. The northern stretch of the enclosing wall and one tower are now reduced to foundations, but the west and east walls still stand. A tower at the north-east angle acted as a strong-point on the perimeter of the outer defences. In the basement of this tower there is an impressive array of arrow-slits covering the north and east walls of the middle ward and the seaward approaches. A latrine tower and a postern gate (the castle's back door) are located in the southern corner of the middle ward.

The final phase of Anglo-Norman work occurred between the years 1226 and 1242. Again this was a building programme designed to add to the defences of the castle. The construction of the outer ward now took the entire promontory within the castle walls. The landward entrance to the castle complex was defended by a huge double-towered gatehouse with two portcullises, still the access used by today's visitors.

The castle was involved in a number of important incidents in the history of Ulster. It was taken by King John in 1210 and in 1315 it was besieged by the invading Scots army of Edward Bruce, brother of Robert. The siege lasted for a year until the beleaguered garrison was forced to surrender. In the rebellion of 1641 it was a refuge for the Protestant inhabitants of the area. Schomberg captured the town and castle from its Jacobite garrison after a siege of one week in August 1689, and William III landed at Carrickfergus in 1690. In February 1760 the town and castle were attacked and captured by a French expeditionary force of 800 men under Commodore Thurot, although their occupation was brief as they departed on 26 February. The castle was used as a prison during the United Irishmen rebellion in 1798,

Fig. 82 Reconstruction drawing of Carrickfergus Castle, harbour and town in about 1620 (Philip Armstrong).

with William Orr and Luke Teeling numbered among the captives confined within its walls.

Guns and gunpowder are first mentioned at Carrickfergus in 1539 during the reign of Henry VIII, and in the 16th century the Anglo-Norman arrow-slits were rebuilt in small 'Tudor' bricks as gunports. Archers continued to be listed among the garrison for several decades, but guns and cannon were growing in importance. Written sources refer to the composition of the garrison and the provision of cannon during the 17th and 18th centuries, and by the 18th century the castle was serving as a barracks and magazine. The early 19th-century threat of a Napoleonic invasion led to the castle being repaired and made ready for war. The double-towered gatehouse was lowered and vaulted to transform it into a pair of 'Martello' towers defended by cannon. After the danger from France had passed the castle was less important but continued in use as a military depot until the early 20th century. Its last call to duty was in the Second World War when it was used as an air raid shelter for the people of the town.

It is hard to point to a clearer example of continuity of use than Carrickfergus Castle. The strategic location proved to be well chosen, commanding important routes by land and sea. As methods of warfare changed and expectations of domestic comfort increased the fabric of the castle was adapted, and Tom McNeill has identified no fewer than ten main building periods, from the late 12th

Fig. 83 Aerial view of Carrickfergus Castle, harbour and town.

to the 19th century. Military use continued for about 750 years and though the castle's life as a fortress has ended it now serves as a rich resource for the town, for visitors to Carrickfergus and for schoolchildren, an impressive reminder of eight centuries of Ulster's history.

Other historic monuments in Carrickfergus include St Nicholas's Church, parts of which date from John de Courcy's time, and the substantial early 17th-century town walls (J 415876 and area).

McNeill, T E, *Carrickfergus Castle* (HMSO, Belfast, 1981), Northern Ireland Archaeological Monographs: No 1; *Carrickfergus Castle* (Belfast, 1992), DOE NI guide-card.

19. DUNDRUM CASTLE | Co Down

J 404369

NW of Dundrum, on a wooded hill overlooking the village. There is a car-park downhill from the castle.

Fig. 84 Dundrum Castle, Co Down: gatehouse, upper ward and keep.

The castle is prominently sited on a rocky height above the village of Dundrum. This hilltop location provides the visitor to the castle with splendid views of the inner bay at Dundrum, the surrounding countryside, and the Mourne Mountains. It was for this reason that the site was chosen by the Anglo-Normans as a centre for strategic control of their newly-conquered lands. Anyone travelling by land into east Down had to pass near to the castle on their journey. The castle also protected the sheltered tidal inlet at Dundrum and its adjoining coastline from seaborne invasion.

The Anglo-Normans were not the first to exploit the natural defences of this rock. In 1950 archaeologists exca-

vated and discovered a pre-Norman bronze roundel and drystone structures on the hill. The nature of this occupation remains uncertain but it is clear that the hilltop was settled in the Early Christian period. The Irish name for Dundrum (*Dún Droma*) means 'the fort on the ridge'.

The castle complex is in two sections - an upper and a lower ward. The upper ward on the hilltop was the centre of the Anglo-Norman castle, and it is likely that John de Courcy (see *Feature 10*) built a defended enclosure here soon after his arrival in the north in 1177. This temporary fort, probably of timber and earth, was soon replaced by an oval enclosure defended by a stone wall formed of connecting straight lengths of walling. Deep ditches were quarried into the rock to provide the summit with added defensive strength. The original entrance into the castle was by a narrow gap in the eastern section of the curtain wall, protected by a drawbridge across a rock-cut pit, still visible as you enter the upper ward.

The circular keep in this ward is three storeys high, quite different in design from rectangular keeps like the one built by de Courcy at Carrickfergus (see this chapter). The corners of rectangular keeps proved to be vulnerable to undermining, and circular towers represented a strategic advance. Circular keeps are not common in Ireland but they are found in south Wales and the Welsh border. Adventurers from this region took a prominent part in the invasion of Ireland and they may be responsible for bringing the new design. De Lacy replaced de Courcy as the Anglo-Norman lord in Ulster in the early 13th century, and he may have constructed the stone keep at Dundrum to replace an earlier timber tower. Excavation in 1960 showed that a pit was cut into the rocky floor of the keep to collect water by seepage, so providing the tower with a supply of water.

Fig. 85 Dundrum Castle: keep in upper ward.

The badly ruined gatehouse belongs to the later 13th century, probably having been built at sometime in the 1260s to replace the more vulnerable old entrance. This century saw the Anglo-Normans concerned with the strengthening of many of their castle defences. A gatehouse was also added to Carrickfergus Castle. The gatehouse at Dundrum consisted of two square towers flanking a central entrance passage. The eastern tower had a semicircular projecting tower to block the new approach up a rocky ramp from the west. Timber buildings, perhaps a hall, a chapel, a kitchen and stables,

would have been present behind the protecting walls of the upper ward.

In the later Middle Ages the castle passed into the hands of the Irish Magennis family. They remodelled the keep in the 15th century, providing a new door and rebuilding the upper parts of the keep. The clearest sign of this late medieval Irish work is the wickerwork centering (see Chapter 9: Audley's Castle) visible in the window openings in the upper parts of the keep. The lower (13th-century) openings show the marks of plank centering. While we do not know for sure when the lower ward was added to the castle, it was probably during the time of the Magennis occupation. The polygonal lower ward, entered from the west, took in a greatly increased area on the lower slopes of the hill. In the far south-west corner of the lower ward is a house added by the Blundell family in the 17th century. Structurally of two phases, it is now L-shaped in plan. With its wide windows and tall chimneys it would have been in stark contrast to the grim Anglo-Norman stronghold on the hilltop. The house lacks any defensive features and was clearly very much a residential building. Note the scars of decorative triangular pediments over the windows facing south.

Fig. 86 Dundrum Castle: 17th-century house in lower ward.

While we remain uncertain about the nature of the Early Christian period activity on the hilltop, it is certain that the rocky ridge at Dundrum was chosen for its strategic advantages, and the place-name element *dún* often points to a site of considerable local importance. John de Courcy and his Anglo-Norman successors recognised the natural strength, progressively adding more advanced defences as the nature of warfare changed, and this process continued under Magennis control in the later Middle Ages. The latest structural phase, the 17th-century Blundell house, illustrates the change so tellingly expounded by Martyn Jope in 1960, from fortification to architecture. The defences of the lower ward were breached, the large, well-lit house was designed for comfort rather than defence, and there are hints of architectural elaboration of some elegance. The house does not appear to have had a long life, and by the 18th century the ruins of the castle were a popular subject for antiquarian illustrators. The slopes of the hill were planted with trees, probably in the 18th century, so that the keep now appears from a distance above the woodland - picturesque, but only in the imagination is it the dominating military stronghold it was for 800 years or more.

Waterman, D M, 'Excavations at Dundrum Castle, 1950', *Ulster J Archaeol* 14 (1951), 15-29; Jope, E M, 'Moyry, Charlemont, Castleraw and Richhill: fortification to architecture in the north of Ireland', *Ulster J Archaeol* 23 (1960), 97-123; Waterman, D M, 'The water supply of Dundrum Castle', *Ulster J Archaeol* 27 (1964), 136-9; *An archaeological survey of Co Down* (HMSO, Belfast, 1966), 207-11; *Dundrum Castle* (Belfast, 1982), DOE NI guide-card.

---

20. DUNEIGHT   Motte and Bailey   Co Down   J 278608

3.8 km S of Lisburn and 1 km E of Ravernet. Parking at the roadside is restricted and requires care.

The visitor to Duneight will see a large, grassy, earthwork with an impressive profile. A tall, flat-topped mound stands to the west, triangular in plan with very steep sides. The mound is separated from a lower platform by a deep ditch. This platform has a truncated oval plan and is surrounded by a bank and ditch, with a further ditch to the east. On the south side the ground falls away sharply to the Ravernet (or Ravarnet) river.

The Anglo-Norman advance into east Ulster in 1177 was followed by the construction of many fortifications. Although the stone castles, like Carrickfergus and Dundrum, may now be a more familiar symbol of the Anglo-Norman presence, in fact most of their fortifications in east Ulster were simpler and less expensive structures of earth and timber. These earthworks are known as 'mottes'. They took the form of steep-sided earthen mounds, resembling a child's sandcastle, with a timber hall or tower on top and wooden palisades around the summit providing additional defence.

Duneight is a good example of one of these earthwork castles, built by the Anglo-Normans at some time between 1177 and 1230 to control the river valley. However, an excavation conducted in 1961 showed that the site had a history of occupation that predated Anglo-Norman activity in Ulster.

During the later part of the Early Christian period - the 10th to 12th centuries - the site was chosen for the construction of an oval earthwork enclosure. This stronghold had banks and ditches on three of its sides but on the south the steep natural slope to the river below was considered sufficient for defensive purposes. The annals refer to a *Dún Eachdhach* in the years 1003 and 1010. In the latter entry the fort (*dún*) and town (*baile*) are recorded as having been destroyed by Cenél Eóghain forces. *Dún Eachdhach* may be the enclosure fortress of Duneight. The excavations recovered slight traces of buildings to the east outside the fort. Could these flimsy structures be the remains of the town destroyed in 1010? The identification of this site with *Dún Eachdhach* of the annals is tempting, but not completely certain.

Roughly a quarter of Irish mottes were accompanied by defended courtyards, known as 'baileys', adjoining but on a lower level than the mottes. Whereas a stone castle could take many years to complete, a motte could be built fairly quickly. In order to economise in time and effort, the Anglo-Normans sometimes built their earthworks on pre-existing Irish raths or even prehistoric mounds, and this was the case at Duneight. The defences of the old fort were remodelled and repaired, and the motte was added over the west end of the old enclosure. The remaining internal area of the enclosure was reused as the castle bailey, but a deep defensive ditch was dug to divide it from the motte.

Fig. 87 Duneight Motte, Co Down.

Fig. 88 Reconstruction drawing of a motte.

Duneight was not the home of a lord like John de Courcy; it would have been garrisoned by ordinary soldiers. In common with many other mottes in Antrim and Down, it was positioned in the border region between Anglo-Norman territory and neighbouring Irish kingdoms. Duneight stands guard over the Ravernet river valley and was built to provide strategic protection for the Anglo-Norman settlements of the Down plateau against any attack launched by the Irish kingdoms from the west. There are no documents to tell us about life at Duneight, and finds from the excavation were scanty, but work elsewhere, as at Clough Castle, Co Down, has produced a clear picture of domestic life in the castle, including evidence for the presence of three or four cats!

This ridge beside the river was attractive long before the period of the visible earthworks. The 1961 excavation in the bailey uncovered parts of a Bronze Age urn with a cremation and two flint tools. In this case there is no question of continuity, and there was no trace of activity again until late in the Early Christian period. The substantial earthwork enclosure of this period may have been an important regional headquarters, and the Anglo-Norman invaders certainly recognised the strategic importance of the site, remodelling it for their own use. The castle is now a grassy mound, but the house at its foot to the west, and Duneight House to the south-east, remind us of the long history of occupation in this riverside location.

Other motte and bailey castles include Clough (J 409403) and Dromore (J 206531), both in Co Down, and Harryville, Co Antrim (D 112026).

Waterman, D M, 'Excavations at Duneight, Co Down', *Ulster J Archaeol* 26 (1963), 55-78; McNeill, T E, 'Early castles in Leinster', *Journal of Irish Archaeology* 5 (1989-90), 57-64; O'Conor, K, 'Irish earthwork castles', *Fortress* 12 (1992), 3-12.

21. INCH ABBEY | Co Down | J 477455

1.2 km NW of Downpatrick, approached from a turning W off the A7 and down a lane to a car-park at the entrance to the site.

Fig. 89 Aerial view of Inch Abbey and the river Quoile, Co Down.

The ruins of the abbey lie on the north bank of the river Quoile in a hollow between two drumlins. Originally this was an island (Irish *inis*) in the Quoile marshes. The extent of the marshes in the past can be seen on the first (1834) Ordnance Survey map for the area and the visitor crosses a causeway to reach the site. Despite its island location, however, the abbey was not isolated from the outside world. It was easily reached by water and was close to the important town of Downpatrick.

The first monastery at this site was in existence by AD 800 and was called *Inis Cúscraidh*. The large precinct of this monastery was defined by an earthwork enclosure

which can be traced partly on the ground and partly by using air photographs. On the ground, the early bank and ditch can be followed along the line of trees on the east boundary of the site, and in part along the west boundary. The buildings of the early monastery would have been made of timber and we can imagine the same range of wooden structures as at Devenish and Nendrum in their earliest phases (see Chapter 6), including church, refectory, houses, guest-house, workshops, and agricultural buildings as well as gardens and orchards.

Inch was attacked by Vikings in AD 1001 and it was plundered again in 1149. It is not certain what kind of settle-

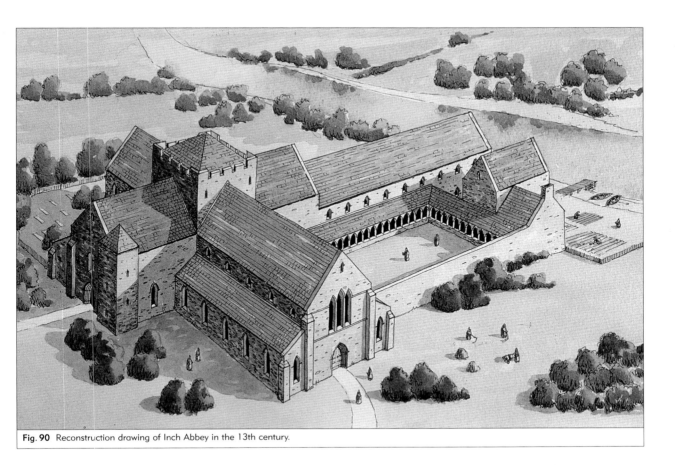

Fig. 90 Reconstruction drawing of Inch Abbey in the 13th century.

ment survived at the site in the mid 12th century, but it is likely that some form of religious presence remained in 1177 when John de Courcy began his invasion of Ulster (see *Feature 10*). De Courcy was a very religious man and he founded several monastic houses in Ulster. He invited Cistercian monks from Furness in Cumbria to establish a new monastery at Inch, and it is said that he built Inch in reparation to God for his destruction of the abbey of Erenagh in Lecale during warfare. The Cistercian monastery was located near to the river in the southern area of the Early Christian earthwork enclosure.

The Cistercian ruins are approached along a path to the west end of the abbey church. Inch follows a standard Cistercian plan, with a cruciform (cross-shaped) church, an aisled nave to the west, two projecting transepts, each with two chapels, and the unaisled chancel to the east with its elegant triple pointed windows (lancets) and distinctive open scaffolding holes. The plan is now complicated by the insertion of walls closing off the

chancel from the nave and the north transept from the crossing. The nave of Cistercian churches was reserved for the use of the lay brothers who followed a less austere regime than the monks and did much of the heavier work. A wooden screen would have closed off the nave from the monks' choir and chancel further east. There was an altar in each of the rib-vaulted transept chapels, and in the north transept is a door out to the monks' cemetery (no longer visible) and a tower with a broken stair in the north-west angle. A number of incised symbols can be seen on the stone plinth of the north transept's exterior north wall. The symbols (called masons' marks) identified the work of each mason engaged in the construction of the abbey, possibly to assess the quality of their work or to establish which mason would receive payment for a particular section of work. The east end of the church, the chancel or presbytery, was reserved for the priests (presbyters) officiating at services. The high altar was under the east windows, and in the south wall (to the right) are the remains of triple sedilia, seats for the priest and his assistants, and a piscina for washing the vessels. If you look closely you will see that much of the detail in the chancel is made up with cement over decayed sandstone, restoration carried out in the 19th century.

South of the church is the cloister, an open court surrounded by buildings which in Cistercian abbeys followed a fixed plan all over Europe. This is in marked contrast to the planning of earlier Irish monasteries, like Devenish and Nendrum, and must have represented a major break with earlier tradition. Unfortunately, the cloister walk, the covered way with an open arcade towards the central cloister 'garth', is missing at Inch and a considerable effort is needed to imagine it, providing access to all the buildings round the cloister. Along the east range from the south transept are a vestry for storing service equipment, a small chapter house where the monks met every day for the reading of a chapter of their rule and to discuss disciplinary and other matters, a small parlour, the only room where the monks could enjoy a conversation (from French *parler*, to talk), and finally a long day room which was used for various indoor activities. The monks' dormitory ran over the east range, with access by a night stair to the church for night-time services. Along the south side of the cloister are the foundations of the refectory and kitchen. The covered walkway would have continued along the west and north sides, but a small excavation in 1993 on the west side of the cloister failed to uncover the foundations of any stone buildings in this area. South-east of the cloister is a long low foundation close to the river, perhaps an infirmary for the care of the sick and aged, while to the west is a well and a bakehouse with two ovens. A low rectangular foundation further south has a doorway towards the river.

The foundation date of the abbey is not entirely secure: it is 1180 in one source but 1187-8 in another. The style of the architecture in the church, distinctively Gothic, indicates a start date of about 1200, so it seems that temporary buildings were first used. It is also possible that there was already a stone church on the site which could be reused, because one Romanesque carved stone of 12th-century date has been found at the abbey. The community of monks was probably never very large (the small chapter house suggests this), and this may have led to a decision to reduce the size of the church by walling off a smaller area to the east end. It is interesting to note that some continuity was maintained with the 13th-century work by reusing a fine door of that period as the

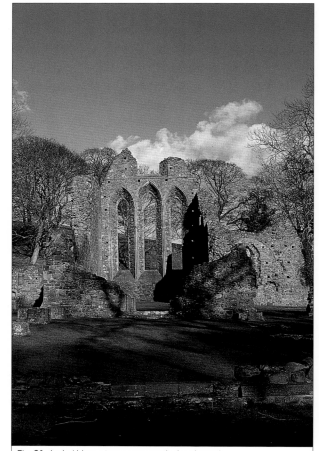

Fig. 91 Inch Abbey: view east towards the chancel.

west door of the reduced church. Monastic life continued, probably on a small scale, to the 16th century, but the abbey had been dissolved by 1541, when its lands were granted to Gerald, Earl of Kildare.

Cistercians did not allow lay people to worship in their churches but they often provided a chapel just outside the monastery for the laity. In the papal taxation of 1302-6 a chapel at Inch is assessed separately from the abbey, and it is likely that this chapel was in the area of the parish graveyard, north of the abbey, where remains of a church survived until the 19th century. During the monitoring of a dredging scheme a number of worked oak timbers were recovered from the river Quoile at Inch in 1991 and 1992 by a team of IUART divers (see *Feature 14*). Two of the beams were dated by dendrochronology (see *Feature 7*) to the mid 16th century. The beams may have been part of a bridge or a jetty, perhaps constructed to aid in the removal of material from the abbey after its dissolution, or perhaps to facilitate access to the chapel which continued in use for Church of Ireland parish worship until 1730. After that date a new church was built at Ballynacraig though, as is often the case, burial continued at the old site.

Many Cistercian foundations were in remote locations, 'in places far removed from the conversation of men', as the Cistercian statutes laid down, but at Inch there had been a church or monastery on the bank of the Quoile for many centuries before the arrival of the Cistercians in Ireland in the 1140s. The Gothic architecture and the Cistercian way of life introduced by monks from Cumbria represented a very sharp break with the past, and there are indications that Inch was on poor terms with its Irish neighbours. So here we find elements of both continuity and change: continuity of ecclesiastical use, extending to continuing burial in the parish graveyard to the present day, but abrupt changes in religious life and architecture in the late 12th century and in the 16th-century church with the dissolution of the abbey and the subsequent Protestant use of the church and graveyard north of the abbey ruins.

Other Anglo-Norman foundations include Cistercian Grey Abbey (J 583682), Augustinian Movilla Abbey (J 504744) and (formerly Benedictine) Down Cathedral (J 482445), all in Co Down.

Hamlin, A, 'A recently discovered enclosure at Inch Abbey, County Down', *Ulster J Archaeol* 40 (1977), 85-8; *Inch Abbey* (Belfast, 1983), DOE NI guide-card; Stalley, R, 'Irish Gothic and English fashion', *The English in medieval Ireland* (Dublin, 1984), ed Lydon, J F, 65-86; Stalley, R, *The Cistercian monasteries of Ireland* (London, 1987).

FEATURE 10 JOHN DE COURCY

Fig. 92 Reconstruction drawing of de Courcy's castle at Carrickfergus in about 1200.

The Normans were the descendants of Vikings who settled Northern France (Normandy) in the 10th century and were soon incorporated into French society. Excellent warriors, they pioneered new military techniques including the use of heavy cavalry and the construction of castles. Using these methods of warfare, they expanded beyond their homelands to conquer new territory from the 11th century onwards, arriving in England in 1066. A century later Normans in Britain - Anglo-Normans - were invited to

come to Ireland to help the king of Leinster, Dermot MacMurrough, in his wars with neighbouring kingdoms. The Anglo-Normans who arrived in Ireland in 1169 were a mixture of French, Flemish, Welsh and English. They responded to Dermot's invitation because they saw a chance to create new lordships and estates for themselves in Ireland.

One ambitious young Anglo-Norman was John de Courcy, younger son of a family connected both with Cumbria and Stogursey

(Stoke Courcy) in Somerset. He had probably journeyed to Ireland with Henry II in 1171 in the hope of securing an estate for himself. A tradition records that the king granted him a licence to conquer Ulster, but since the Ulster kingdoms were very strong at this time, we may perhaps see any such grant from Henry as a joke at John's expense. De Courcy is next heard of in 1177 leading a small force of 22 knights and 300 foot-soldiers into the north on a four-day march. He arrived in Downpatrick at the beginning of

February, forcing Rory MacDonleavy, king of the Ulaidh, to flee.

Recent research has identified that John had many contacts with the north of England, southern Scotland and the Isle of Man, and that his associations with these areas would have provided him with the necessary access to the soldiers and supplies required for his invasion to succeed. This in turn would suggest that he had carefully pre-planned his actions, though it is possible that he may also have received aid from some disgruntled party within Ulster society. For the next five years he fought off all attempts to oust him made by the northern kingdoms. The Ulaidh, the Cenél Eóghain and the Cenél Conaill made an alliance to get rid of the stranger in their land, and in 1178 they nearly suceeded: de Courcy and his men were ambushed in north Antrim and only just managed to escape on foot after all their horses were killed in the fight.

In the writings of his contemporary, Gerald of Wales (Giraldus Cambrensis), we are told that John was fair-haired, tall, lanky and very strong. He was a brave warrior, always in the thick of the battle, rallying his men behind him, wielding his two-handed sword and scattering his foes before him. It seems that he was a clever man as well. To give an air of legitimacy to his conquest of north Down and south Antrim he enlisted the help of (or perhaps even invented) an old prophecy which stated that a conqueror of Ulster would come forth who had a device of birds on his shield. John displayed painted eagles on his shield to 'fulfil' the prophecy.

A Cenél Eóghain raid on Ulaidh territory in 1182 brought to an end the alliance against de Courcy. After this date there are no references to John fighting against the Ulaidh people. It seems that he now became their ally against the other Ulster kingdoms, becoming self-styled 'Master of Ulster' while the MacDonleavys remained Ulaidh kings. He underlined his new role by following the Ulster royal tradition of marrying the daughter of the king of the Isle of Man, Affreca, in about 1180.

Fig. 93 De Courcy farthing from Muckamore Priory, Co Antrim.

John not only built many castles in his territory (see this chapter: Carrickfergus and Dundrum) but, as Gerald records, he 'gave the church of Christ that honour which is its due'. He founded new monasteries (see this chapter: Inch, and also Chapter 6: Nendrum) and was a generous patron to the church. In 1185 he was given the important job of taking charge of the administration of Henry II's affairs in Ireland as Justiciar, remaining in the post probably until 1189. De Courcy's position must have seemed totally secure; he had integrated himself fully into Ulster society as a new, apparently acceptable, political force and had created a strong lordship for himself. Who could have predicted that in a few years all his work would be overthrown?

The events surrounding John's fall from power are obscure. He may have been considered a threat to the royal power of King John in Ireland or he may have fallen out with his one-time comrade in arms, Hugh de Lacy. At Downpatrick in 1204 he was beaten in battle with de Lacy and was banished from his Ulster lordship. On 29 May 1205 King John granted de Lacy the de Courcy lands in Ulster and made him an earl. Attempts by John de Courcy to reverse this setback by military action failed and in 1207 he was given permission by the king to return to England. He later seems to have taken service under the monarch, since he was back in Ireland at the king's side in 1210, and in 1216 he was fighting French forces which had invaded England. It seems he was dead by 22 September 1219 when a mandate was issued giving Affreca a widow's share of her late husband's property. As far as we know, the adventurer and his wife had no children, although a Patrick de Courcy is mentioned as the tenant-in-chief of Cork in 1221. This man established the Kinsale de Courcy family line and while some connection with John is probable, history remains silent on the relationship.

Orpen, G H, *Ireland under the Normans*, 4 volumes (Oxford, 1911 and 1920, reprinted 1968); Gerald of Wales, *Expugnatio Hibernica* (Dublin, 1978), ed Scott, B, and Martin, F X; McNeill, T E, *Anglo-Norman Ulster* (Edinburgh, 1980); Duffy, S, 'The first Ulster plantation: John de Courcy and the men of Cumbria', *Colony and frontier in medieval Ireland: essays presented to J F Lydon* (London, 1995), ed Barry, T, Frame, R, and Simms, K, 1-27.

Fig. 94 Audley's Castle, Co Down (Infra-red photograph by Tony Corey).

Chapter 9
Late Medieval Ulster

1.2 km SW of Newtownstewart, approached across a field from the minor road to Rakelly on Gallows Hill.

Harry Avery's Castle stands on a high hill overlooking the town of Newtownstewart and commanding an important complex of river valley routes. From a distance the castle seems to look like the double-towered gatehouse which defends the entrance to Carrickfergus Castle (see Chapter 8). However, a closer inspection of the ruins shows that any resemblance is restricted to appearance and does not extent to function.

The entrance to Harry Avery's Castle is between two massive D-shaped towers. A screen wall originally connected the rear of the towers at a high level but collapsed in the early years of this century. In the south-west face of the doorway is a square draw-bar slot. Excavation in 1961 showed that a pear-shaped bridge-pit lay outside the entrance, so access to and from the castle would have been provided by a lifting bridge, and a series of holes in the faces of the D-shaped towers may be connected with the machinery needed to lift the bridge.

The entrance leads to a ground floor chamber, formerly covered by a vault but now open to the sky. Note that there is no access at this level to the courtyard or bailey,

but from the south-west corner a stair led to the first floor room above. This was a hall, originally roofed in timber, and off it there are two small chambers with window-seats in the two D-shaped towers. In these, and in several other places, there are clear signs of the wicker centering on which the vaults were built (see this chapter: Audley's Castle). Stone chutes survive showing that there were latrine chambers at both first- and second-floor levels. Access to the courtyard was only from this first-floor level, so it is clear that the masonry structure is not a gate-house but rather a massive defensive and residential tower fronting a raised bailey.

The bailey is a natural knoll of glacial sand and gravel which has been artificially shaped to create an elevated courtyard, enclosed and protected by a strong, polygonal curtain wall. Though the wall is now ruined to a low level, projecting wall towers have been found along the north-west and north-east sides, but no gateway has yet been discovered and this suggests that the 'gatehouse' provided the only means of entry to the bailey. Timber buildings may have stood inside the bailey but any trace of them was destroyed by later agricultural activity on the knoll.

Fig. 95 Harry Avery's Castle, Co Tyrone, in the early 20th century, Green Collection, WAG 384 (Ulster Folk & Transport Museum).

It is important to imagine what Harry Avery's Castle looked like when the curtain wall stood to its full height with at least two projecting wall towers. The sandy knoll would have been entirely cased in masonry and the castle would, superficially, have looked very much like an Anglo-Norman stone castle with gatehouse and walled bailey, like Carrickfergus Castle. Harry Avery's Castle does, however, represent a development from the earlier castles with their separate halls and functional gatehouses. Here the hall and gatehouse are amalgamated into one compact, self-contained unit, an arrangement which has more in common with tower-houses of the 15th and 16th centuries (see this chapter: Audley's Castle) than the stone castles of the 12th and 13th centuries.

The location of Harry Avery's Castle, in the heart of Gaelic Ulster, indicates that it was built by an Irish lord. It is obvious that he had been influenced by what he had seen at Anglo-Norman castles, but it is also clear that the design and construction of the building were carried out by Irish craftsworkers. One sign of this is the use of wicker centering for vault construction. The 'Harry Avery' after whom the castle is named was Henry Aimhréidh ('the Unsmooth') O'Neill, who died in 1392. During the 13th and 14th centuries the O'Neills and O'Donnells came into conflict over the land of west Tyrone. The O'Neills gained strategic advantage by building a castle here since it overlooks the junction of three rivers and important routes in the disputed territory. The castle does not seem to figure in any 15th- or 16th-century documentation for the area, which suggests that it may not have been considered an important stronghold by that time. The strong traditional association with Henry Aimhréidh O'Neill, the similarity in appearance with the gatehouses of the 13th and 14th centuries and the silence of the 15th-century documentation all suggest that Harry Avery's Castle is of 14th-century date.

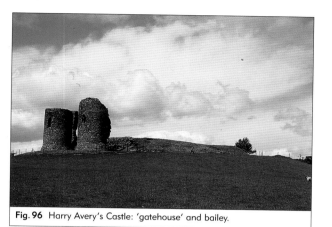

Fig. 96 Harry Avery's Castle: 'gatehouse' and bailey.

mound known as Pigeon Hill, a raised rath, indicating that the river valley was an area of activity in the Early Christian period. Uphill from Pigeon Hill, on the ridge overlooking the river, is the early 17th-century castle at the head of the street of the Plantation village (see also Chapter 10: Bellaghy Bawn), with its English-style chimneys and Scottish crow-stepped gables. These three defensive and residential structures at Newtownstewart symbolise both continuity and change, spanning a thousand years, from the Early Christian period mound, through the exotic O'Neill stone castle, to the fine Plantation castle with its imported Scots and English features.

The useful life of Harry Avery's Castle was probably fairly short, but it can be viewed as an element in the wider historical landscape of this strategically important area. Close to the old bridge in Newtownstewart is an oval

Jope, E M, and H M, and Johnson, E A, 'Harry Avery's Castle, Newtownstewart, Co Tyrone, Excavations in 1950', *Ulster J Archaeol* 13 (1950), 81–92; Meek, H, and Jope, E M, 'The castle at Newtownstewart, Co Tyrone', *Ulster J Archaeol* 21 (1958), 109–12; Rees-Jones, S G, and Waterman, D M, 'Recent work at Harry Avery's Castle, Co Tyrone', *Ulster J Archaeol* 30 (1967), 76–82.

23. DUNLUCE CASTLE | Co Antrim | C 904414

On the A2 coast road between Portrush and Bushmills, with a car-park at the entrance.

Undoubtedly the most spectacularly sited castle in Ulster, the ruin of Dunluce clings to a promontory of basalt battered on three sides by the roaring ocean. Writing in 1584 Sir John Perrott described the castle as 'the strongest piece of this realme, situate upon a Rocke hanging over the sea, divided from the main with a brod, deepe, rocky ditch, natural and not artifical, and having no way to it but a small necke of the same rocke, which is also cutt off very deep'. These natural defences had made this promontory a natural choice for protected settlement from Early Christian times onwards. The name Dunluce includes the fort element *dún*, and a rock-cut souterrain (see Chapter 7: Drumena) is located on the north-east side of the site.

On arrival the visitor first passes through the mainland court, with its ruined stables, smithy and lodgings, all probably of late 16th- or 17th-century date. In the adjoining field to the west of this court can be seen terraces which once formed part of a landscaped garden.

In the 17th century this part of the castle complex became the main settlement area; the second Earl of Antrim's wife, the Duchess of Buckingham, preferred to live on the mainland since she did not like the noise of the sea.

The strong walls of the mainland court converge to the north to form the 'Funnel', the only route to the main body of the castle. The medieval stone castle on the promontory is not recorded in surveys of the 1350s and may have been built by the MacQuillans who were the lords of the region from the late 14th or early 15th centuries. In the 16th century the area was colonised by the Scottish MacDonnells, who moved into north Antrim after losing land to the Campbells in Argyll and Islay. It is largely their buildings that survive today.

Some form of drawbridge originally spanned the chasm that divides the mainland from the promontory. A

Fig. 97 Aerial view of Dunluce Castle, Co Antrim - 'the strongest piece of this realme'.

splendid gatehouse with Scottish-style corbelled-out turrets guards the entrance. It is of late 16th-century date and was probably built by the MacDonnells to replace an earlier gatehouse destroyed by Sir John Perrott's artillery in 1584. Attempts by the English government to expel the Scots from Ireland proved futile. Under their exceptional leader, Sorley Boy, the MacDonnells resisted attacks from the O'Neills and English forces. Dunluce was captured by Shane O'Neill in 1565 and by Perrott in 1584, but on each occasion the MacDonnells subsequently resumed occupation.

The large, round north-east and south-east towers and their connecting wall belong to the earliest phases of the castle. The remaining buildings in the upper and lower yards all date from the MacDonnell years of occupation. The upper yard is dominated by the early 17th-century hall (the last building to be constructed on the promontory) with its large bay windows (one restored) and fireplaces. The construction of this hall obscured an earlier feature, an open gallery (called a loggia) along the south wall where people could sit or walk. Only a row of column bases of this structure survives.

The lower yard with its original cobbled surface contained servant accommodation and domestic buildings. The north range may have been the scene of a disaster in 1639 when part of the building collapsed into the sea below, carrying a number of servants with it. This tragedy may have led to the abandonment of the promontory in favour of the mainland court. Under the castle is a sea cave which served as a natural harbour where Scottish galleys could be landed. A crude carving of one such galley on a stone is displayed at the castle in the Visitor Centre.

In the later 17th century the castle was abandoned by the MacDonnell family who then moved to nearby Ballymagarry. The one-time bustling town that existed to the south and west of the castle decayed and vanished except for earthwork traces in the fields. It is recorded that the town was burnt in the conflict of the 1640s, although its Scottish inhabitants were allowed safe passage to leave and go back to Scotland. The ruins of the town's old church still stand and Hill records that the oak roof was removed and used for a barn in the vicinity. The names of the inhabitants of the town and surrounding countryside who lie at peace in the graveyard are mostly

Fig. 98 Dunluce Castle: Scottish-style gatehouse.

The jagged outline of Dunluce Castle reminds us of Ulster's many-layered history, from the defended *dún* of the Early Christian period, through the complex family conflicts of the Middle Ages and the wars of Queen Elizabeth's reign, to the mixed Scottish, English and European Renaissance influences of the 17th century. The abandonment of the castle and disappearance of the 'town', on the other hand, illustrate how settlement patterns can change, and how defensive considerations became less important as the 17th century gave way to more settled conditions in the 18th century.

Other north Antrim monuments associated with the MacDonnells include Dunseverick Castle (C 988445), Bonamargy Friary (D 126408) and Layd Church (D 245289).

of Scottish origin and they are largely the same names as the people of the area today. The picturesque ruins of Dunluce Castle became a favourite subject for the artists who travelled to the Causeway Coast in the 18th and 19th centuries, and it is still a popular subject for calendars, book jackets and tourist publicity.

Hill, Rev G, *The MacDonnells of Antrim* (Belfast, 1873); Meek, M, *Dunluce Castle* (DOE NI, 1993); Smith, P, 'On the fringe and in the middle: the MacDonalds of Antrim and the Isles 1266-1586', *History Ireland* 2.1 (1994), 15-20.

Fig. 99 Dunluce Castle: reconstruction drawing of early 17th-century hall and the gatehouse on the promontory.

24. AUDLEY'S CASTLE | Tower-house and bawn | Co Down | J 578506

1.6 km NW of Strangford in the Castleward estate, signposted from the A25 Downpatrick to Strangford road.

Fig. 100 Aerial view of Audley's Castle, Co Down, showing estate houses and Castle Ward house in distance (Barrie Hartwell).

Audley's Castle stands on a rocky knoll overlooking the strategically important waterway linking Strangford Lough with the Irish Sea. From the car-park at the foot of the hill the visitor sees a tall, imposing tower, and on closer inspection the defensive strength of the monument becomes clear. The castle commands magnificent views across to Portaferry, and is protected on its south side by a rocky cliff.

The monument is entered by a gate beside the south-west wall of the tower-house which is on the site of the original entrance to the 'bawn' (a defended enclosure). The stone walls of the bawn here have been reduced to low foundations, but its rectangular plan can still be traced. In the south-east area of the bawn are the foundations of an

outhouse, probably a barn or servants' accommodation, and the tower-house is at the bawn's north corner.

The south-east face of the tower-house is dominated by two projecting square turrets, linked by an arch at parapet level – a machicolation – through which objects could be dropped on anyone attacking the door in the south turret below. The ground floor room is entered through a small lobby which has another defensive device – a 'murder-hole' in its roof, operated from the floor above. The ground floor room is lighted by narrow window loops and has a wall cupboard and a chute for slops.

The south turret contains a spiral stair which leads to the two upper chambers and the parapet. The first floor chamber has a semicircular stone barrel vault, designed as a defence against the spread of fire. A number of beam-sockets and projecting stone corbels in the walls show how the vault was erected. Timber formwork was put in place to support the vault during construction, woven wicker mats of willow or hazel were laid on top and a bed of mortar was poured onto the mats. The stones of the vault were then set in the mortar and more mortar was worked in from above. When the mortar had hard-ened the timber was removed but the wicker mats were left in place and their negative impression can often be seen on the underside of the vault (see also Chapter 8: Dundrum Castle). The presence of window-seats, a fire-place, two cupboards and a latrine (in the east turret) suggests that the first floor chamber was the main living room in the castle.

The second floor chamber lacks a fireplace but it does have window-seats and a latrine in the east turret so it could have been the sleeping area. The latrine may also have been designed to serve as a prison since the door leading into it was closed and secured by a draw-bar from the main chamber. Above this floor is the roof level with a wall-walk behind a parapet and higher corner turrets, now largely demolished. We know that the castle had a pitched roof because a drawing of 1840 shows a gable wall in place which subsequently collapsed. The timber roof of the castle would have been covered with slates, wooden shingles, stone slabs or thatch.

Audley's Castle is probably of 15th-century date, but its early history is unknown. The castle bears the name of its late 16th-century owners, the Audleys, an Anglo-Norman family who held land in this area in the 13th century, but it is not known if they built the castle. It was sold with the surrounding estate to the Ward family in 1646.

Tower-houses are small, fortified castles built and occu-pied by lesser landowners with their families and retainers. While tower-houses may not have had the comforts enjoyed in a modern home it would be wrong to think that they were grim, dank dwellings. What we see today is the shell of what was once a proud, defensive home. Contemporary accounts of life in a tower-house show that when plastered, whitewashed and heated they were greatly superior to the sod-houses or cabins lived in by the majority of the population at the time.

There are some 3,000 tower-houses in Ireland, being most numerous in Munster and Leinster but with many

Fig. 101 Section through a Co Down tower-house, showing chambers at each floor level and spiral stair contained in corner turret.

examples in Down and Donegal. They were built from the 15th century to about 1650 by both Anglo-Norman and Gaelic families, at a time when strong central govern-ment was lacking and there was much unrest in society. They were also built in other contemporary European regions suffering from similar circumstances, such as the borderland between England and Scotland. After the horrors of the Black Death and other disasters in mid 14th-century Ireland much land changed hands and many new lordships were formed. There was also a move from arable to pastoral farming and this generated trade and wealth. The development and spread of tower-houses must be seen in this context of change, new wealth but also insecurity.

Fig. 102 Audley's Castle.

and Jordan's Castle in Ardglass, has been likened to the gatehouses of earlier castles like Carrickfergus and Dundrum, but this is only one possible influence. Another is 13th-century hall-house castles in Ireland, or even influence from abroad.

Tower-houses therefore developed out of a time of change, but once established as a type, useful both in towns, like Carrickfergus and Ardglass, and in the country, as at Audley's, they continued to be built until the mid 17th century. As Ireland became politically more stable tower-houses were superseded by fashionable, spacious and grand country houses. Landowners left the security of the tower for the comfort of the country house. In the case of Castle Ward, the old tower was retained as a feature of a new farmyard, and Audley's Castle served a new purpose as a picturesque landscape feature, viewed across an artificial lake, Temple Water, created when the predecessor of the present Castle Ward house was built in the early 18th century. The end of the tower-house as the main form of residence for landowners in Ireland is explained by its lack of purpose in a changed society, though Audley's Castle found a new role as an element in an elaborate 18th-century designed landscape.

Other tower-houses in Co Down include Kilclief (J 597457), Jordan's Castle in Ardglass (J 559372), Quoile (J 497470), and Strangford (J 589498). Examples of tower-houses in Co Antrim include Dunseverick (C 988445) and Olderfleet at Larne (D413016).

An archaeological survey of County Down (HMSO, Belfast, 1966), 225-7; *Three tower-houses: Audley's Castle, Strangford Castle, Portaferry Castle* (HMSO, Belfast, 1980), DOE NI guide-card; McNeill, T E, 'The origins of tower-houses', *Archaeology Ireland* 6.1 (1992), 13-14; Donnelly, C J, 'Frowning ruins: the tower-houses of medieval Ireland', *History Ireland* 4.1 (1996), 11-16.

By the later Middle Ages the big Anglo-Norman stone castles like Carrickfergus and Dundrum (see Chapter 8) were less important than in earlier years, but did they influence the design of tower-houses in any way? The distinctive elevation of Audley's Castle, with the two projecting turrets and linking arch, seen also at Kilclief

FEATURE 11   ANIMAL BONE STUDIES

The bones of mammals, birds and fish are a common discovery on archaeological excavations, usually representing the discarded, disarticulated and butchered remains of meals long ago. As such, these bones can tell us much about the diet and economy of the people who lived at a particular site in the past. It is important for the osteoarchaeologist (see *Feature 4*) to collect all available information present in these disarticulated remains so that the maximum amount of economic and dietary knowledge can be gained from an animal bone assemblage.

The osteoarchaeologist's first task in the laboratory is to divide the bone fragments from each archaeological layer or feature into separate groups which contain the bone fragments from each single species. The majority of bone fragments from a site are those of large domesticated animals - cattle, sheep, goats and pigs. The specialist then sorts through the bone fragments for each species so that he or she can calculate how many animals the fragments represent. It is necessary to record which parts of each bone are present and whether they are from the left or the right side of the body. In this way it is possible to estimate the minimum number of individuals (MNI) in an assemblage.

As is the case for the osteoarchaeologist working with human bones (see *Feature 4*), the animal bone specialist is also interested in estimating the age and sex profiles of the various species of animal recovered from a site. Only some bones

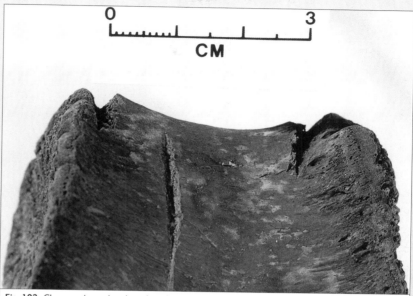

Fig. 103 Chop marks on butchered cattle vertebra (Eileen Murphy).

of the body are useful for determining the sex of an animal. Male pigs, for example, have tusks which are larger than their female equivalents. In addition, certain features of the pelvic bones and differences in the size of other bones (such as cattle metacarpels) may enable the sex of an animal to be determined. It is possible to obtain an estimate of the age at death of an animal by examining the stages of development of each bone and the stages of tooth eruption and tooth wear. Animal remains can also provide us with information about the butchering tools and techniques employed in the past. By examining the size and shape of butchery marks on a bone it is possible to tell the type of tool which was used. The location of butchering marks can also indicate how a carcass was sectioned, while the position of the marks can indicate if the body was skinned.

Although animal remains are generally recovered in a fragmentary condition it is still possible to obtain information about animal health in the past from a study of the palaeopathological lesions present on bone fragments. The presence of a degenerative bone disease may indicate if an animal was used for pulling heavy carts or for ploughing. Examples of trauma include raised, smooth areas of bone (ossified haematomas) found on the lower leg bones of cattle. This injury may suggest that the animals were being housed together in cramped conditions where they were liable to kick each other.

The excellent waterlogged conditions at the inner ditch of the Late

Bronze Age hillfort at Haughey's Fort, Co Armagh, (see Chapter 5: Navan Fort) provided a major source of information on the farming economy practised in prehistoric times. Cattle were the predominant animal encountered in the sample and the majority of the beasts were of a small breed, though at least two individuals were extremely large suggesting that they may have been the result of selective breeding. A large proportion of the animals were mature and semi-mature when they were slaughtered and this indicates that a beef economy was probably in operation. Pigs were of secondary economic importance and, while the majority were domesticates, the bones of wild pigs were also identified. Although very few sheep or goat remains were found at the site, suggesting that they were of limited importance to the hillfort dwellers, the presence of two very long goat horns may again indicate that selective breeding practices were in operation. Very large dog skulls have also been discovered - including the largest dog skull identified in the archaeological record for the British Isles. The inhabitants of the hillfort seem to have kept massive hounds, perhaps for hunting or for use as guard dogs.

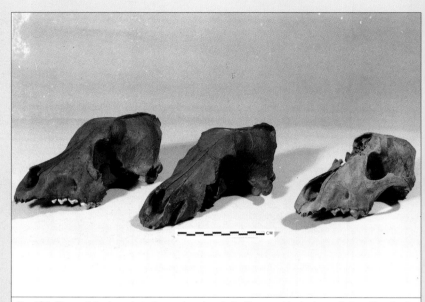

Fig. 104 Three of the large Late Bronze Age dog skulls discovered in the inner ditch at Haughey's Fort, Co Armagh (Barrie Hartwell & Eileen Murphy).

Cat skeletons from rural contexts of Early Christian date indicate that the animals were generally well cared for, with large stature and a long life expectancy, perhaps suggesting that they were kept as valued pets. In contrast, Viking Age and medieval urban cat skeletons from Dublin had a shorter life expectancy and were generally smaller. In addition, a number of cat skulls from 13th-century levels in Dublin displayed cut marks suggesting that they may have been skinned for their pelts, a theory which finds support in the documentary sources for the period.

McCormick, F, 'The domesticated cat in Early Christian and medieval Ireland', *Keimilia: studies in medieval archaeology and history in memory of Tom Delaney* (Galway, 1988), ed Mac Niocaill, G, and Wallace, P F, 218-28; Rackham, J, *Animal bones* (London, 1994); Murphy, E M, and McCormick, F, 'The faunal remains from the inner ditch of Haughey's Fort: third report, 1991 excavation', *Emania* 14 (1996), 47-50.

FEATURE 12 TOWNLANDS

The townland is the smallest unit of land division in Ireland. All other territorial units - counties, baronies, parishes - are formed from amalgamations of townlands. Originally Irish, but later anglicised, the townland name for an area normally highlights natural (hills, rivers, oakwoods) or artificial (churches, fields, settlement) features in its composition. Estimates of the number of townlands in Ireland vary between 60,000 and 70,000. Anglo-Norman documents record place-names which have survived to modern times as townland names, and the townland seems to have been in use from at least the 12th century. The same place-names may have been used and passed down by word of mouth from generation to generation in Early Christian Ireland.

Ulster Gaelic lords needed to be able to control the land they ruled over, since in medieval times land equalled wealth. In order to achieve this their territory was divided into large land units called 'ballybetaghs', which were then subdivided in different regions into 'polls', 'tates' or 'bally-boes'. A modern townland usually equals one of these subdivisions in size. Each unit of land could be assessed for tax according to its size or value. A clan could be given control of a land division as its own estate, held collectively by the extended family group and passed down from one generation to the next. Some estates were connected to hereditary posts in Gaelic society; we have already seen that the O'Hagans were hereditary guardians of Tullaghoge and that they held land in the surrounding area (see Chapter 7).

In the aftermath of the Plantation the old system of land control was replaced. While the larger Gaelic land units were abandoned, however, the smaller units were fitted into new territorial divisions such as counties. It is the small land units which became the townlands. During this period their Irish names were written down phonetically by English scribes who changed them into the anglicised versions of their original names that we use today.

In the new social organisation of the landscape the townland played an important role which enshrined it in the legal documentation and maps of the day. Policing divisions, electoral boundaries, land valuations and census returns all operated by townland. It was used by rural communities to identify where they lived or what farm they worked. Families who lived in a townland often became associated with its name in

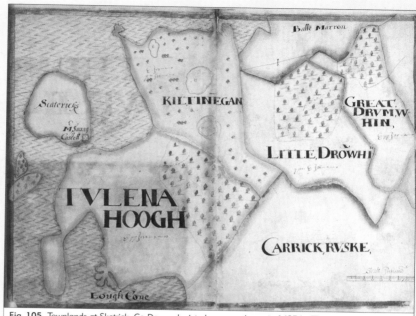

Fig. 105 Townlands at Sketrick, Co Down, depicted on map drawn in 1625 by Thomas Raven (PRONI).

order to distinguish them from other families in a district with the same surname. Nor is the townland only to be found in rural areas. As towns expanded in the 18th and 19th centuries into their surrounding countryside the old townland names were retained for the new settlements. Malone, Stranmillis, Shantallow, and Creggan are a few examples of urban townland names.

For the archaeologist townland study can be of importance if the townland name incorporates the name of an ancient settlement type, such as 'cashel', 'rath' or 'Kill' (church), perhaps long since vanished from the area. Townland data can also be used to correlate early 17th-century land grants with the modern landscape.

The everyday use of our townland names ensures that this important living element of our heritage will continue to survive. In 1973 the Post Office in Northern Ireland adopted a policy of naming rural roads, numbering houses along them and assigning postcodes for greater efficiency. Where implemented, this system threatened to lead to the disuse of townland names by the people who lived in them. The loss to our heritage would have been appalling. Fortunately, in the face of strong opposition, the Post Office agreed to accept the inclusion of the townland as part of the full postal address for any premises in Northern Ireland. The townland is an enduring reminder of the continuity of use of our landscape through the centuries by successive generations. It forms a direct line of contact between ourselves and our past.

McErlean, T, 'The Irish townland system of landscape organisation', Landscape archaeology in Ireland, British Archaeological Report 116 (1983), ed Reeves-Smyth, T, and Hamond, F, 315-39; Canavan, T, Every stoney acre has a name: a celebration of the townland in Ulster (Belfast, 1991); Mac Shamhráin, A S, 'Placenames as indicators of settlement', Archaeology Ireland 5.3 (1991), 19-21.

Fig. 106 Derryloran Old Church, Co Tyrone (Infra-red photograph by Tony Corey).

Chapter 10

The Plantation

12 km SSW of Newry, approached by minor roads, under the railway bridge and along a short path.

Moyry Castle stands on a rocky height overlooking the 'Gap of the North', the Irish *Bealach an Mhaighre*, one of the most important ancient routeways into Ulster. The castle is a square tower with unusual rounded corners inside a walled enclosure or bawn which is only partly preserved. The tower is entered by a door in the north-east wall, protected by a gun-loop and a parapet projection (machicolation) through which missiles could be dropped on any unwelcome visitor. The ground floor has no domestic comforts but is well-provided with gun-loops. The two rooms above were clearly the living quarters, with fireplaces and windows. A wall-walk at the top gave access to further gun-loops, the machicolation and a latrine.

This is clearly an austere defensive structure, far more seriously military than a tower-house like Audley's Castle (see Chapter 9). It dates from the time of the Elizabethan wars in the late 16th and early 17th centuries, when the English armies were advancing north into east Ulster (see *Feature 13*). The route through the pass here was very treacherous, through dense woods, across streams and on causeways through bogs, terrain where, according to one

observer, 'the Irish might skyppe but the English could not goe'. The Irish harried and delayed the Crown forces, and the English commander, Lord Mountjoy, realising the immense strategic importance of the pass, put in hand the building of Moyry Castle in 1601. He called on a Dutch engineer to supervise the work (the employment of Continental experts was quite common at the time) and it was apparently completed in the month of June 1601. It was garrisoned at once by Captain Anthony Smith and twelve men, but it is not known for how long the castle was occupied and defended.

Although Moyry Castle may have had a short military life, the route which it was built to command amply illustrates the theme of continuity. Close to the castle, down-hill, is the Early Christian ecclesiastical site of Kilnasaggart with its inscribed pillar stone datable to about AD 700. Kilnasaggart lies on the 'main road', the *Slighe Mhiodhluachra*, which ran north from Tara to Dunseverick in north Antrim, one of the five great roads of Early Christian Ireland. Close to Moyry, on a nearby hilltop, is a stone fort, Lissacashel, also of the Early Christian period, which in its day also watched over the pass. We know

Fig. 107 Moyry Castle, Co Armagh.

Fig. 108 Moyry Castle: detail of map by Richard Bartlett in about 1601 (National Library of Ireland).

from a poem about Edward Bruce that he rested at Kilnasaggart on his way to Dundalk in 1318, clearly using the route through the pass.

This route through the mountains between Newry and Dundalk has continued to be important to the present day. The railway line from Belfast to Dublin runs close to Moyry Castle and from the castle you can see the line running north across the plain towards Newry. Only a little further away is the main road between Newry and Dundalk which also runs through the 'Gap of the North'. Moyry Castle therefore symbolises a period of change, when English forces were advancing north into Ulster in the early 17th century, but the route which it was built to control has been important for well over a thousand years.

Davies, O, 'Moiry Castle', *Proceedings of the Belfast Natural History and Philosophical Society* 1.4 (1938–9), 31–8; Hayes-McCoy, G A, *Ulster and other Irish maps c.1600* (Dublin, 1964), 2 and plate I; Kerrigan, P M, *Castles and Fortifications in Ireland 1485-1945* (Cork, 1995), 54.

26. DERRYLORAN OLD CHURCH | Co Tyrone | H 805768

The ruin of Derryloran Old Church stands in its graveyard above the Ballinderry River, close to a bridge and the A505 road to Omagh, on the south-west outskirts of Cookstown.

Fig. 109 Derryloran Old Church, Co Tyrone, showing 18th-century porch and bell-cote.

The name Derryloran points to an early origin for a church here: *Daire Lúráin* means 'the oak wood of Luran', and Luran's festival day is listed as 29 October in a calendar of saints dating from just after AD 800. There is a reference in the annals to the plundering of Derryloran and other churches in the vicinity in 1195. Nothing survives on the site from this early period, and it is possible that all the early buildings were made of wood.

There is evidence in the surviving ruin of the next period of building activity. Many pieces of carefully dressed sandstone are reused in the east and north walls, including distinctive roll mouldings, probably from a

13th-century door. So here we have evidence for the medieval parish church of Derryloran, which succeeded the Early Christian church and was listed as *Dilirulan* and valued at two marks, 4s and 2d (a mark was 13s 4d, the equivalent of 66p in modern money) in a papal taxation roll of 1302-6. The names of many of the parish priests are known from the late 14th to mid 16th centuries.

The church we see today dates from the Plantation period in the early 17th century. After a period of bitter warfare and disruption of society in the late 16th century the medieval church was probably ruined, but when Allan Cook leased this area from the Archbishop of Armagh in about 1609 he reused the old site for his

109

Fig. 110 Derryloran Old Church: east window.

probably date from the 18th century, when other changes were made. A fine stepped entrance to the grave-yard was created, and a porch and bell-cote were added to the west end of the church. This work may have been done during the mid 18th century, when William Stewart MP was developing the present town of Cookstown with its imposing wide main street.

The old church remained in use until 1822, and much plaster can still be seen on the interior walls from this late period, but it clearly was inconveniently sited on the outskirts of the town and was eventually abandoned for a new church in Cookstown. The graveyard remained in use and there are two particularly imposing memorials. Adjoining the east end of the north wall of the church is the massive tomb of the Stewart family of Killymoon, erected in 1680 and repaired in the 1840s, while inside the church in the south-east corner is the tomb of Henry Lewis von Stieglitz of Gortalowry House, who died in 1824. Fifteen years ago the ruin was shrouded in dense ivy and the east gable was in danger of total collapse, but the DOE NI's Historic Monuments staff carried out a difficult programme of conservation which was finished in 1988.

Fig. 111 Derryloran Old Church: east gable undergoing conservation in 1983.

new Protestant parish church to serve the nearby village – the first 'Cookstown'. A survey of 1622 describes the church as 'almost complete'. Excavation has shown that the medieval walls were demolished to ground level and used as the footings for the new church.

The ruin is a long, narrow structure, with an east window with plain intersecting tracery. This had to be removed and restored during recent conservation work, and the new work can be easily distinguished from the old. In the north wall are a blocked window and door, perhaps blocked in an attempt to fortify the church in a period of insecurity, or to counter some structural problem. We know that Allan Cook's settlement was destroyed in the 1641 rebellion. A single projecting stone in the outer wall-face near the blocked door may remain from a porch. The two more westerly windows in the south wall are different from those further east, and they

This has been a place of worship and burial for well over a thousand years. The founding saint of the 6th or 7th century gives the parish its name. Traces of the medieval parish church can be seen in the walls of the Plantation period successor, while burials in and around the church may span more than 1,200 years. This long sequence at Derryloran reflects both continuity and change, and it is repeated at many ancient church sites throughout Ulster.

Other Plantation period churches include Benburb, Co Tyrone (H 817522), Derrygonnelly Old Church, Co Fermanagh (H 120524), St John's, Island Magee, Co Antrim (J 464979) and, the finest, St Columb's Cathedral in Derry City.

Davies, O, 'Derryloran Church', *Ulster J Archaeol* 5 (1942), 8–11; Brannon, N F, 'Five excavations in Ulster, 1978-1984', *Ulster J Archaeol* 49 (1986), 89-98.

27. DUNGIVEN PRIORY AND BAWN — Co Londonderry — C 692083

Reached on foot down a long path from the A6 (main Belfast to Derry road) at the SE approach to Dungiven.

Fig. 112 Dungiven Priory, Co Londonderry: view from scullery east to nave.

The ruined church stands in a large graveyard on a promontory overlooking the River Roe. There are steep slopes on the west and south sides, but a gentler approach can be made from the east. The naturally strong site suggests that the people who used it over many centuries had at least an eye on its defensive aspects.

Early written sources associate a saint called Nechtán with Dungiven, and he was thought to have come from *Alba* (Scotland). Nothing more is known of the Early Christian period church, but it is believed to have occupied this site. The ruined church which the visitor now sees shows work of many periods, indicating a

Fig. 113 Dungiven Priory: O'Cahan's tomb in chancel.

two bays, and the vault was apparently remodelled in the 15th century, when a fine new window was inserted in the north wall of the nave. The chancel would have been furnished with an altar and wooden stalls. The quality of the work in the chancel suggests highly skilled craftsmen and generous patronage, and this impression is confirmed by the splendid tomb against the south wall, Dungiven's most famous feature. An armed figure in a quilted garment lies under a canopy of openwork flamboyant tracery, with six small attendants standing guard on the arcaded front of the tomb. There is nothing else like it in the north, but it does closely resemble late medieval tombs in the Western Highlands of Scotland and it is possible that it is the work of a Scottish mason. Dates in the late 14th and the 15th century have both been suggested.

The tomb is traditionally the burial place of Cooey-na-Gall O'Cahan, who died in 1385. We know that the church was under the patronage of the O'Cahan family who dominated this area from the late 12th century onwards, and the fine chancel clearly reflects this. The nave, however, may date from before their dominance. At some point in the 12th century the old church connected with Nechtán was refounded as a priory of Augustinian Canons, a pattern found all over Ireland, and it was this priory that the O'Cahans patronised so generously. The O'Cahan tomb reminds us of the strong links which Derry diocese had with the Western Highlands, and especially Iona, throughout the Middle Ages.

The substantial foundations visible west and south-west of the nave belong to two secular structures: an Irish tower-house (see Chapter 9: Audley's Castle) and an English-style manor-house of the early 17th century. Attached to the west end of the nave is the foundation of a squarish tower which stood in part until about 1800. The tower's stair was square below but circular above and some people have claimed that this was an early round tower. Recent research has made it clear, however, that it was part of the O'Cahan tower-house, added to the west end of the church at some point in the later Middle Ages.

South and west of the tower-house foundations are other walls, of a stone-flagged scullery reached down steps and a long range with a large base for two fireplaces. These foundations were excavated in 1982-3 as the culmination of a programme of research which overturned long-held theories and threw new light on the use of the site. It was well known that the English garrisoned Dungiven in 1602 and that Sir Edward Doddington had built a substantial house

long and complex history – just how complex has only become clear in recent years.

The earliest part of the stone church is the nave which originally stood alone. At its north-east corner is an unusual feature: three raised horizontal bands run across the east wall from a slight angle pilaster, perhaps echoing timber construction. Two other features survive from the early church. The distinctive semicircular-headed window in the south wall is identical to a window in nearby Banagher Church, and the remains of a blind arcade on the interior face of the east wall, interrupted by the later chancel arch, has decorated capitals clearly of the 12th century.

The chancel was added in the 13th century and is very carefully detailed, inside and outside. It is lit by a pair of tall, narrow windows with a niche on each side, all linked with projecting string-courses. The chancel was vaulted in

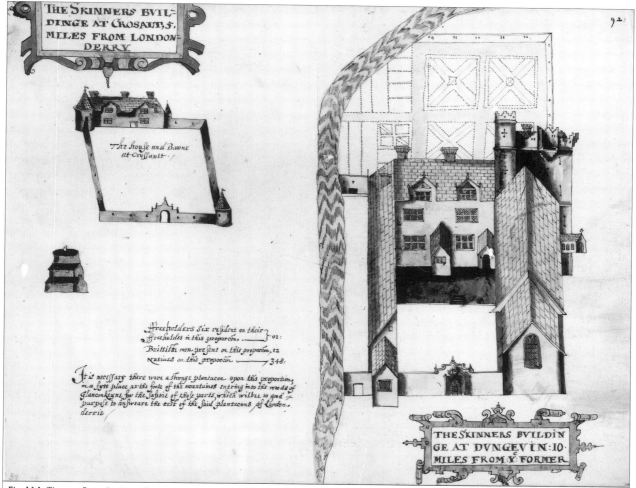

Fig. 114 Thomas Raven's pictorial map of Dungiven in 1622 showing priory, manor-house and bawn (PRONI).

by 1611, but the general opinion was that this activity was at the site of a ruined military post in Dungiven village. Recent research, however, showed that written descriptions of the Plantation complex and pictorial sources, like Thomas Raven's drawing of 1622, must refer to the priory site and, when that was realised, several other pieces of the puzzle fell into place. Sir Edward Doddington refurbished the church for Protestant worship, and the present chancel arch and the porch on the north side of the nave clearly date from his time.

Until 1982 there was no sign at all of the manor-house above ground, but the Plantation period sources give the dimensions of the house and the excavation was designed to confirm its existence. Doddington died in 1618 but his widow was still living in the house in 1654.

Excavation showed that the house had been burned down, probably in the late 17th century, but that it had lain empty before the fire. There were plentiful finds of fittings, like locks, hinges and nails, but little domestic material or remains of furnishings.

The church was used for Church of Ireland worship until 1711 but the old site continued in use for burial. The remains of Doddington's house, and the enclosing bawn wall shown in the 1622 illustration, were gradually covered by earth and grass. There are 19th-century accounts of pilgrimages to the site, including stations on the slope down to the Roe, and the continuity of tradition is illustrated by the 'rag tree' beside the path in the graveyard. The thorn bush overhanging a hollowed bullaun stone filled with water is covered with bandages

Fig. 115 Dungiven Priory: excavation of manor-house scullery in 1982.

uing use of the site for burial today. Cutting across this continuity is the break with tradition represented by the end of the priory's life at the Reformation in the mid 16th century, and the taking over of the site previously occupied by the Augustinian Canons and the O'Cahans by Doddington and Protestant worship. Recent research has elucidated this long history, and the excavation has allowed the physical remains of the O'Cahan and Doddington structures to be displayed and understood, side by side with the priory ruins.

and other strips of cloth, left by visitors seeking a cure (see also Chapter 6: Ardboe, and Chapter 11: Struell Wells).

At Dungiven, therefore, it is possible to trace continuity of activity probably from the Early Christian period and certainly from the 12th century through to the contin-

Brannon, N F, and Blades, B S, 'Dungiven Bawn re-edified', *Ulster J Archaeol* 43 (1980), 91-6; Brannon, N F, 'Archaeological excavations at Dungiven Priory and Bawn', *Benbradagh* 15 (1985), 15-18; *Dungiven Priory and Bawn* (Belfast, 1986), DOE NI guide-card; Brannon, N F, *Pieces of the past* (HMSO, Belfast, 1988), ed Hamlin, A, and Lynn, C J, 81-4.

Footnote: A partition now closes off the chancel from the nave to protect the medieval tomb from vandalism and weathering. Visitors wishing to enter the chancel should make prior arrangements with the DOE NI Environment and Heritage Service (see p 5).

28. TULLY CASTLE   Co Fermanagh   H 126566

4.8 km N of Derrygonnelly, reached by a lane from the A46 Enniskillen to Belleek road and a turning to a car-park.

Situated on the highest point of a hill overlooking Lower Lough Erne, Tully is a fine example of a Plantation castle of the early 17th century. The ruins consist of a house and a bawn with a rectangular tower (flanker) at each corner, designed for hand-gun defence. The flankers were stone roofed and the presence of fireplaces suggests that they were used for accommodating servants or guards. The bawn was entered through a gateway in the south wall, and the house lies on the north side of the bawn. It is T-shaped in plan and two stories high, with gun-loops giving defensive strength to a building which resembles a substantial farmhouse rather than a true castle.

In the early years of the 17th century many similar castles and defended homes were built by English and Scottish settlers in Ulster. This was because the Plantation scheme (see *Feature 13*) stipulated that in each land-grant of 2000 acres a castle and bawn had to be built to protect a new

estate. The land at Tully was granted to the Scottish settler Sir John Hume in 1610, and the castle was built by 1613. There is documentary evidence for a Plantation village near to the castle where 24 families lived. After Sir John died in 1639 his son Sir George inherited his estates, but in the rebellion of 1641 the castle was attacked on Christmas Eve by Rory Maguire. Lady Mary Hume surrendered, but this did not prevent a massacre taking place on Christmas Day. Only the Humes were spared, while the castle was put to the torch.

Tully Castle was taken into State Care in 1974 and a programme of conservation was begun. The dense ivy that shrouded the walls was removed and the structure was secured. Excavation revealed a series of paved paths in the bawn including a path from the bawn gateway to the house and, outside the gateway, south to the lough and west to where the village may have been. There was no

Fig. 116 Tully Castle, Co Fermanagh, and recreated 17th-century garden.

Fig. 117 Tully Castle in 1976, before conservation.

evidence of any buildings in the bawn and it seemed likely that the area within the paths had been laid out as a garden.

The house shows architectural features of both Scottish and Irish origin. The T-shaped plan is of a type found at early 17th-century Scottish castles, as are the projecting turrets on the north wall at first floor level. However, while it seems that the design of the building was based on Scottish models the construction was clearly carried out by Irish masons. The ground floor room has a wickerwork centred barrel vault of Irish type (see Chapter 9: Audley's Castle), while the projecting turrets were modified by the Irish builders. Instead of being carried on cut-stone corbels (as at the Scottish-style gatehouse at Dunluce

Castle and at Monea Castle), here they were supported on rubble cones smoothed over with mortar. Finally, the thatched roof that once covered the building was of a kind commonly found on Irish houses at the time.

Tully provides a stark example of discontinuity: the castle was deserted after a life of only about 30 years, and the Hume family moved south-east to Castle Hume where now only the stable yard survives from their 18th-century

115

Fig. 118 Aerial view of Tully Castle showing bawn, flankers and garden.

house a small display. The garden in the castle bawn is a recreation, not a restoration, for no plant remains were discovered during the 1970s excavation, but since 1988 Philip Wood has created a garden in the spaces between the paved paths using only plants known to have grown in Ireland in the 17th century. So, through the work of conservation and display, Tully is brought to life again in the late 20th century.

Other Plantation castles include Ballygalley, Co Antrim (D 373078), now part of a hotel, and Old Castle Archdale (H 186599), Castle Balfour (H 362336) and Monea (H 164493), all in Co Fermanagh.

house. The small cluster of houses south-west of Tully Castle, perhaps the successors of the Plantation village, was occupied until the middle of this century, and one house has recently been restored to receive visitors and

Jope, E M, 'Scottish influences in the north of Ireland: castles with Scottish features, 1580-1640', *Ulster J Archaeol* 14 (1951), 31-7; Waterman, D M, 'Tully Castle', *Ulster J Archaeol* 22 (1959), 123-6; *Tully Castle* (Belfast, 1984), DOE NI guide-card.

| **29. BELLAGHY BAWN** | Plantation bawn | Co Londonderry | H 953963 |

On a hilltop on the southern edge of Bellaghy.

Bellaghy Bawn stands at the southern end of the main street of the village of Bellaghy. From the entrance a path leads into a courtyard, enclosed on three sides. A long, whitewashed two-storey house stands on the south side, connected to a large round tower in the south-east corner. In the south-west corner is a small tower, built of red brick and square in shape. Two houses are attached to the outside of the east wall.

The complex, multiperiod monument that the visitor sees today had its origins in 1619. During the Plantation this area was allocated to the Vintners' Company (wine dealers) of the City of London. Sir Baptist Jones rented the land from the Company and he was responsible for the building of the bawn, originally called Vintners' Hall. The bawn was designed to provide the new community of settlers with a refuge in the event of an attack. Jones constructed a well-defended enclosure and in Pynnar's survey of 1619 he is commended for the speed with which he had completed the task.

Pynnar's survey and a second report by Sir Thomas Phillips in 1622 provide written descriptions of the buildings in the bawn, and a picture map of the bawn by Thomas Raven accompanied the 1622 survey. The bawn was square in plan and had two circular towers at diagonally opposite corners. Two two-storey stone houses stood in the bawn, one on the south side and the other along the west wall, each attached to one of the circular corner towers. The north wall of the bawn, including the gateway into the enclosure, was demolished long ago, but the other three walls are of 17th-century date, though much patched. The large house on the south side is substantially of late 18th-century date and must lie over the foundations of the original two-storey house, the principal 17th-century residence shown on Raven's map. The stout, circular flanking tower in the south-east corner is certainly the tower depicted by Raven, built of locally-produced red brick on a stone footing. The small, square tower of brick in the south-west corner of the bawn is not a Plantation period building: the square tower shown

Fig. 119 Bellaghy Bawn, Co Londonderry.

in this corner in Raven's drawing may have been a wooden structure which was replaced at a later date by the present brick tower.

Bellaghy Bawn came into State Care in 1987 and in 1989-90 Nick Brannon undertook a series of excavations to elucidate the structural sequence and aid the conservation work. Excavation along the west bawn wall located a 17th-century earthen gun platform revetted with stone sealed inside a larger, mid 18th-century platform which was probably part of a landscaped garden. Removal of rubble and a substantial depth of garden soil revealed the inner face of the west bawn wall. This wall had developed an alarming outward lean and had parted from its stone foundations. The excavation showed that this had been caused by building the wall on the fill of a rath ditch (see Chapter 7: Rough Fort, Risk). While it is sometimes the case that settlers made use of earlier earthworks for defensive purposes (see Chapter 7: Tullaghoge), it is likely that Jones was unaware of the ancient settlement on the site. He probably chose the hilltop because it overlooked the site for the new settlement of Vintners' Town (now Bellaghy).

North of the platform the foundations of the Plantation period house, shown in Raven's picture map along the west bawn wall, was uncovered. It was a two-roomed structure, the rooms separated by a large H-plan fireplace. The house appears to have been deliberately levelled at some time during the course of the 17th century. At the north end of the excavated house traces of the stone footings and angled doorway of the north-west circular flanking tower were located. The Raven drawing of 1622 and a map of 1760 show two circular towers at the south-

Fig. 120 Bellaghy Bawn: round tower at south-east corner and outbuildings before conservation.

east and north-west corners of the bawn, but the north-west tower is missing from a map of 1814. Excavation suggested that the tower had been used as a rubbish tip before its demolition at some time between 1760 and 1814. The two houses attached to the outside of the east bawn wall seem to have been built in the 18th century.

Sir Baptist Jones died in 1624 and his property was released to Henry Conway. Despite its obvious strength the bawn was surrendered to, and slighted by, the Irish insurgents of 1641. It was reoccupied in the later 17th century and the house was lived in until 1987 - a remarkable example of continuity of occupation over a very long period. This activity in turn brought many changes to the fabric of the building and its surroundings. The western house may have disappeared before the end of the 17th century, and the 18th century saw the remodelling of the main house and the gun platform, the building of the

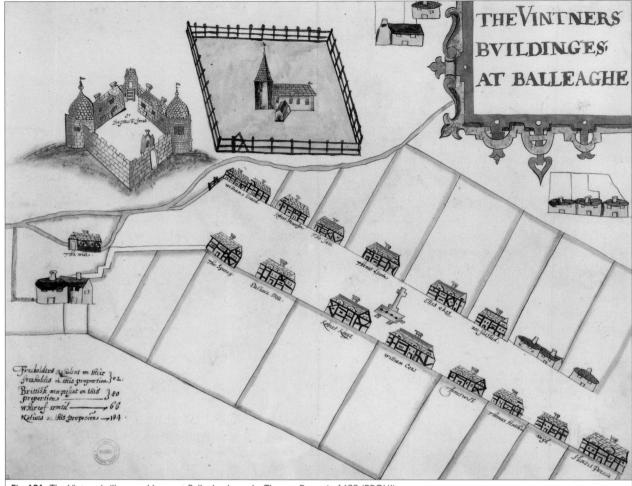

Fig. 121 The Vintners' village and bawn at Bellaghy drawn by Thomas Raven in 1622 (PRONI).

square brick tower and the two houses outside the east wall, and perhaps the demolition of the north-west circular tower. There were further changes in the 19th century, as well as attempts to patch and support the leaning west wall of the bawn over many years. It was not until the 1989-90 excavations, however, that it became clear that the site had been occupied by an Early Christian period rath, demonstrating once again that the factors which influenced siting a thousand years ago still appealed to strategists in the early 17th century.

Other Plantation bawns include Tully Castle (this chapter), Brackfield Bawn, Co Londonderry (C 511096) and Dalway's Bawn, Co Antrim (J 443914).

Jope, E M, 'Moyry, Charlemont, Castleraw and Richhill: fortification to architecture in the north of Ireland, 1570-1700', *Ulster J Archaeol* 23 (1960), 97-123; Brannon, N F, 'Bellaghy Bawn', *Excavations 1989* (Bray, 1990), 16-17; Brannon, N F, 'Bellaghy Bawn', *Excavations 1990* (Bray, 1991), 21.

FEATURE 13 PLANTERS AND GAELS

By the end of the 16th century Ulster was the last stronghold of Gaelic society in Ireland. It had remained outside the sphere of influence and authority which the English government had established elsewhere in the country. The earlier medieval Anglo-Norman colony, in the east of the province, had through time become assimilated into native society and was no longer in a position to act as a bulwark to protect English interests in the north. Political power in Ulster was held by a number of separate Gaelic lordships. Some lordships were more powerful than others, but no individual lordship was of sufficient strength to gain power over all of its neighbours. This resulted in a politically fragmented society that lacked a central authority with absolute control. The principal lordship was that of the O'Neills in mid-Ulster, and a less powerful group was the O'Donnells in what is now Co Donegal. Each had a variety of lesser lords under him who were the leaders of kin-groups (or septs). The lesser lords paid tribute and submitted to the authority of the overlord in return for the right to hold power over an area. In Gaelic society the power of the overlord derived from command over land and people, but land was held collectively by each kin-group.

The lesser lord provided food for his overlord's table and he was expected to provide soldiers and contribute to the payment and billeting of mercenary forces, sometimes from Scotland. He also had to supply labourers and craftspeople to work on the overlord's fields and buildings. Each kin-group had its own role within society. For example, the O'Quinns were sheriffs to their overlord, the O'Neill, while the O'Donnellys were the same overlord's marshals, responsible for the collection of his tribute (see also Chapter 7: Tullaghoge). The lowest ranks of the population had no legal rights within this social framework, but they were given protection and had the freedom to move to the territory of another lord if they were discontented with their lot. Cattle were the major source and gauge of wealth in the economy, often being used in trading or bartering transactions. Cattle also provided milk, meat and hides for everyday use, while cereals such as wheat, barley and oats were grown for local consumption. In coastal regions there was a fishing industry, and the O'Donnell of Donegal exported herring and salmon to Europe in exchange for wine. Horses, hides and linen yarn were also traded with Spanish, French and Scottish merchants in return for wine, clothing and munitions.

The event that heralded the end of the established social framework of late medieval Ulster was the savage war that was fought by the O'Neills and the O'Donnells against the English in the years from 1594 to 1601. The Irish lords took up arms against the forces of Elizabeth I because they viewed their way of life to be under threat from English expansionist policies. Despite early victories on the Irish side the war was won by the English after they defeated their opponents at Kinsale in 1601. A peace settlement was accepted by O'Neill and O'Donnell in 1603 by which they were allowed to keep their land under the titles of tenants-in-chief to the Crown. Elsewhere, Irish freeholders dependent on the Crown for their position replaced the old lords as landowners. The division of Ulster into nine counties (first proposed in 1585) was now carried out, and in order to strengthen the power of the Crown in Ulster it was decided that settlers from Britain should be brought in to populate certain areas.

Neither Hugh O'Neill nor Rory O'Donnell came to terms with their changed positions in post-war Ulster society. English officials, envious that the pair still held their lands, continually harassed them and persecuted them for their Roman Catholic faith. Added to all this was a genuine fear of arrest on the charge of being traitors. On 4 September 1607, therefore, they and their followers sailed from Rathmullan to voluntary exile in Europe, an event known as the 'Flight of the Earls'. The Crown immediately confiscated their lands and drew up a plan that six counties should be colonised by trusted Irish freeholders. However, an unsuccessful Gaelic rebellion in 1608 led the English government to decide that the only way to keep Ulster at peace was to end the favourable treatment of Irish landowners. A scheme of 'Plantation' was published in 1609 and further modified in 1610. This scheme set aside only a small area of each county for deserving 'natives'; the rest of the

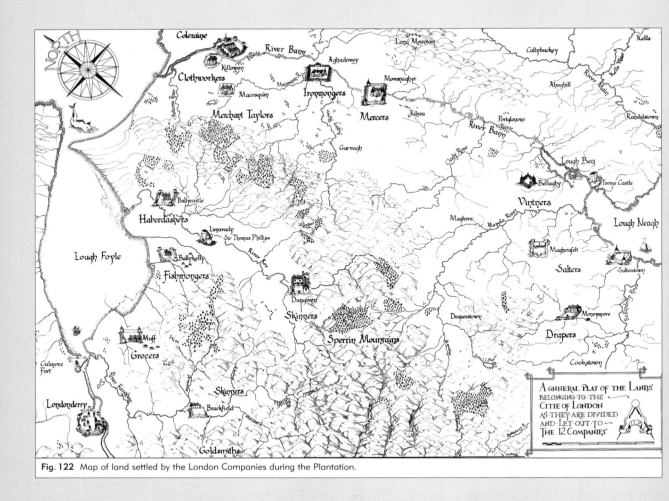

Fig. 122 Map of land settled by the London Companies during the Plantation.

territory of the six counties of Donegal, Tyrone, Coleraine (later renamed Londonderry), Armagh, Cavan and Monaghan was now to be settled with trusted English and Scottish 'Planters'.

Other Plantations had been attempted elsewhere in Ireland by the Crown during the 16th century but had failed owing to a lack of financial or human support. The new Plantation was intended to avoid the mistakes of the past. It was planned to be a systematic, large-scale venture supported in part by the companies of the City of London. The vast majority of the native population was to be removed from the land. Land was to be allocated to 'undertakers' in parcels of 1,000, 1,500 and 2,000 acres and the undertaker was to bring in new settlers as tenants, build defended homes, found new settlements, reform agricultural practices and act as the agent of English law and the Protestant religion. The undertakers were to be English soldiers, English and Scottish Planters, and trusted Irish lords. In practice, however, the undertakers did not attract enough people from Britain to make the journey to Ireland; nor did they have the ability or the will to remove all the native population from their land, especially when the Irish were willing to pay high rents to remain in Ulster. As a result the Plantation strategy had limited success since significant numbers of the original population remained within the Plantation areas. It should not be thought, however, that all the Irish were hostile to the changes within society. A demilitarised society left lesser lords free from the expense of providing overlords with military support. The lesser lord now held his land as a tenant at a fixed rent (though this could be very high) and grievances could be taken to a local court of law for legal redress. Many native landowners became progressively anglicised in their outlook on life. It was mainly the members of families who had lost their positions of power with the passing of the old social hierarchy who turned to a life of brigandry or left to seek employment as soldiers on the Continent.

The changes that the Plantation brought about were visible throughout the 17th-century Ulster countryside. New roads were opened, new bridges were built, and English agricultural practices were adopted. The economy became progressively commercialised and surplus grain and cattle were sold in markets, 150 of which were licensed between 1600 and 1640. As the level of trade with the outside world expanded so too did the size of port towns like Carrickfergus, Coleraine and Derry (then renamed Londonderry). In 1637 hides, cattle, beef, horses, sheepskin, tallow, butter, cheese, linen yarn, oats, oatmeal, barley, malt, fish, timber and iron ore were being exported from Ulster, while clothing, tools, food-stuffs, ironmongery, hardware, coal and salt were among the items being imported. New towns were founded throughout the countryside - Moneymore, Cookstown, and Bellaghy being examples. New architectural styles were introduced, usually in the traditional style of the Planter's homeland. The Scots built their defended homes in a distinctive Scottish style, like Monea Castle, Co Fermanagh (H 164493) and Ballygalley Castle, Co Antrim (D 373078), while English architecture can be seen at Castle Archdale, Co Fermanagh (H 186599) and Castle Caulfield, Co Tyrone (H 755626). The Planters were ready patrons of the church and many new churches were built, sometimes on the site of an earlier church, as at Derryloran Old Church, Co Tyrone (see this chapter).

Fig. 124 Castle Caulfield, Co Tyrone.

Fig. 123 Monea Castle, Co Fermanagh.

of the Irish brogue tradition in association with a Plantation assemblage of clay tobacco pipes, imported ceramics and glasswares.

English gradually became the common language of Gael as well as Planter in society and commerce, but a more serious division existed that was not to be overcome so easily: the natives and newcomers were divided by religious beliefs. The Reformation in Britain happened in the mid 16th century at a time when Tudor authority could not be exerted over Ireland. Rather than make war to impose the new religion the English left the Gaelic lords to practise their old religion, and Ireland remained a Catholic country. The Plantation introduced the Protestant church and a substantial Protestant population into Ulster. Needless to say, not all Planters remained Protestant, nor did all native Irish remain Catholic. In every generation people of Planter and Gaelic stock married one another and changed their religion; evidence of this assimilation can be seen from the names of some of our leading politicans. While the population intermarried, however, the religious divisions remained, and to this day the division persists in Ulster.

Archaeological investigations during 1988 and 1989 by Orloff Miller at the site of the abandoned Plantation village of Salterstown in Co Londonderry have indicated the nature of commercial contacts which existed between the newcomers and the native population in the 17th century. The excavation of a home-lot at the south end of the village street shown in Thomas Raven's pictorial map of 1622 produced distinctive Irish pottery and footwear

Robinson, P, *The Plantation of Ulster* (Dublin, 1984); O'Dowd, M, 'Gaelic economy and society', *Natives and newcomers* (Dublin, 1986), ed Brady, C, and Gillespie, R, 120-47; Gillespie, R, 'Continuity and change: Ulster in the 17th century', *Ulster, an illustrated history* (London, 1989), ed Brady, C, O'Dowd, M, and Walker, B, 104-33; Stewart, A T Q, *The narrow ground* (London, 1989); Mallory, J P, and McNeill, T E, *The archaeology of Ulster* (Belfast, 1991), 299-324; Heath, I, and Sque, D, *The Irish wars 1485-1603* (London, 1993), Osprey Men-at-Arms Series, No 256.

Fig. 125 Ballycopeland Windmill, Co Down (Infra-red photograph by Tony Corey).

Chapter 11

Towards the Present

2.4 km E of Downpatrick, signposted on the B1 to Ardglass and reached down a lane to a small car-park.

Struell Wells is located in a sheltered valley in which lies a large triangular green. A gaunt, roofless building stands to the north-west, outside the modern wall that encloses the green. This ruin is a chapel, built in about 1750, but never completed, to replace an earlier chapel on the site. At the far end of the chapel can be seen a stream running in a south-easterly direction. This stream (*sruthar*) gives the site its name, and the curative properties of its water (although now not safe to drink) have made the valley a place of pilgrimage.

Four buildings are aligned along the route of the stream inside the enclosure. A small round building with a domed stone roof, set directly over the stream, is the Drinking Well. The stream continues, running through underground culverts, to a small rectangular stone house near the centre of the green, the Eye Well. This has a pyramidal roof of large stone corbels. The water from both wells was used by people seeking cures from ill-health.

The underground stream runs on to two rectangular buildings in the south-east corner of the green. The larger of the two, with intact stone roof, was the Men's Bathhouse. There is a dressing-room with seats which leads through to the bathhouse where a rectangular sunken tank is reached by steps and filled with water supplied at floor level by a stone channel. There was a moveable sluice to control the water-flow out of the bath. The building's third room, at a lower level and with its own entrance, is the dressing-room used by women pilgrims. The roofless building opposite the door into this room is the Women's Bathhouse. The water enters from a high level and the women must have had drenches rather than baths. The water leaves the bathhouse through a drain in the opposite wall.

The site is traditionally associated with St Patrick who is supposed to have come from nearby Saul to bathe in the waters. There is no historical evidence to support this connection, and all four buildings within the enclosure probably date from about 1600 or a little later. The earliest known reference to Christian activity here is in the papal taxation of 1302-6 where a chapel is recorded. In 1957 some fragments of 13th-century stone windows were discovered, and these probably belonged to this chapel. They can now be seen built into the field wall next to the

Fig. 126 Struell Wells, Co Down, showing ruined chapel on left.

Fig. 127 Struell Wells: drench in Women's Bathhouse.

Drinking Well. Even though there is no evidence, the site may have been frequented in the Early Christian period and the valley may even have been a pre-Christian place of worship. The early church sometimes seems to have adopted the ritual centres of earlier religion for reuse in a Christian context, so that the local people, newly converted, would have less difficulty in accepting the new religion. Iron Age cults centered round springs and streams, as well as stones and trees (see Chapter 6: Ardboe, and Chapter 10: Dungiven Priory), and Struell Wells in this atmospheric valley is a possible site for prehistoric ritual activity.

We do know that Struell Wells has been a centre for pilgrimage since medieval times: a Papal Nuncio writing

Fig. 128 Struell Wells: Eye Well and bathhouses.

and the Friday before Lammas (1 August) to perform penances or hoping for cures. The pilgrimages continued into the 19th century but rowdy disturbances led to the ecclesiastical authorities prohibiting devotional exercises and the wells were subsequently less visited. Nevertheless in the tranquil rocky valley it is quite easy to imagine that the stream has been frequented not just for the 700 years of documented history but back into prehistory.

in 1517 may have visited the site. In 1643 Fr Edmund MacCana noted that the stream had been brought into existence by the prayers of St Patrick. A fuller account of activity at the wells is given by Walter Harris in 1744: large numbers of people went there on Midsummer Eve

Other sites in Co Down associated with St Patrick include Saul mortuary house and cross slabs (J 509463), Raholp Church (J 541479), and the traditional site of Patrick's grave in the cemetery at Downpatrick Cathedral (J 483445).

An archaeological survey of County Down, (HMSO, Belfast, 1966), 310-11; *St Patrick in County Down* (Belfast, 1987), DOE NI guide-card.

31. HILLSBOROUGH FORT — Co Down — J 245586

On an area of rising ground E of Hillsborough town, approached either by a tree-lined avenue from the town square or a lane from the neighbouring Forest Park car-park.

The visitor to Hillsborough Fort will notice at once an obvious combination of military and domestic architecture. The strong stone walls and spear-shaped corner bastions are to be expected at a fortification, but the building in the centre of the north-west wall (which resembles a child's 'toy' fort) and the small, decorative tower crowning the main entrance on the north-east side appear at first sight to be out of place. Moreover, in the fort's interior is a lawn with a curious semicircular sunken ditch. To understand all these features we must look at the site's history.

The monument had its origins as an artillery fort in the mid 17th century. The man responsible for its building was Colonel Arthur Hill, a royalist in the Civil War, who

had shown great pragmatism on the defeat of that cause and had taken up a position in the victorious Parliament under Cromwell. At the Restoration in 1660 he again showed his ability to change allegiance (like a great many of his generation) and became a Privy Councillor to the new king, Charles II. The fort was probably built in the 1650s and was strategically placed on high ground to guard the road from Dublin to Belfast and Carrickfergus. Its importance is clear from the fact that it was made into a royal garrison in 1660, and William III visited the fort on his way south to the Battle of the Boyne in 1690. Hillsborough town may have its origins in the 17th century when a small village grew up near Hill's artillery fortification, but its main growth was from the 18th century onwards.

Fig. 129 The 'gothick' gatehouse at Hillsborough Fort, Co Down.

Fig. 130 A 'coming-of-age' celebration at Hillsborough Fort in 1809.

Hill's fort embodies certain European defensive concepts of the time, developed and tested in the sieges of the Thirty Years War and other conflicts. The fort was laid out as a square with sides 81 m in length, enclosed by earthen ramparts. The outer faces of the ramparts were fronted with stone walls, and these walls were extended up to provide a parapet wall behind which the garrison could man the defences in the event of an attack. At each of the four corners of the fort are spear-shaped bastions, large enough to carry the weight of a heavy cannon, and these bastions provided flanking fire along the walls. In the centre of the north-west rampart was a gatehouse providing a protected entrance to the fort.

The next main phase in the history of the monument was in the mid 18th century when the Hill family transformed the old decaying fortification into a 'gothick' castle where they could hold social gatherings. The old gatehouse was remodelled in the form of a four-towered 'toy' fort, with battlements, large pointed windows and

doorways and grotesque stone heads. The Hills used the first floor of this building to entertain their guests and friends if bad weather prevented events being held on the lawn inside the fort. Mrs Delany (a notable 18th-century traveller) stayed at Hillsborough in 1758 and records that the lawn was laid out as a bowling green and there were plans for each of the bastions to be planted as a garden.

Since the original entrance to the fort had now been reworked to create the 'castle', a new entrance was

Fig. 131 Hillsborough Fort: excavated rath ditch inside the fort.

inserted in the north-east wall, crowned by a gothick tower, or gazebo, with curly sandstone tracery in its wide windows. Lesser openings were also cut through the ramparts on the south-west and south-east sides.

The monument has been in State Care since 1959. During restoration work on the 'castle' carried out in 1968 25 oak floor beams were removed from the building. This was the first major group of post-medieval timbers examined by Mike Baillie when he was constructing his dendrochronological calendar for Ireland (see *Feature* 7). The beams showed signs that they had been used in some other structure before being reused in about 1758 in the construction of the 'castle'. The dendrochronological date for the beams suggested that they were unlikely to have been felled before 1641 at the earliest. Mike Baillie has suggested that they may have been reused from a church known to have been built between 1660 and 1662, replacing one destroyed in the 1641 rebellion, and itself replaced, or rather remodelled, in the 18th century. The present fine Church of Ireland parish church of St Malachi was reopened in 1773 after major remodelling, and the fort was being worked on in 1758 (according to Mrs Delany), so the suggestion is quite feasible.

When the monument was being worked on for public presentation in the 1960s a part of the hidden history of the site was revealed. In the interior of the fort a circular depression was noticed in the lawn. Excavations in 1966 and 1969 showed that this hollow was the largely infilled ditch of an Early Christian rath (see Chapter 7: Rough Fort), and the half of the ditch that was excavated was left open as a reminder of the earlier settlement which once occupied the site. The excavation suggested that the old rath ditch may have been reused as a defensive base while the artillery fort was being built in the mid 17th century. After the fort's construction was completed the bank of the rath was presumably demolished and the ditch was filled in to create a flat parade ground in the centre of the new fort.

Just as at Bellaghy Bawn (see Chapter 10), and doubtless many other places, strategists coming to Hillsborough in the 17th century looking for a strong, defensible position chose the site of an Early Christian period rath. This had probably been abandoned as a settlement 600 or more years earlier, but it may have provided temporary shelter before being lost under the up-to-date military architecture of the 17th-century fort. When the defensive life of the fort came to an end, the Hill family transformed it into a pleasure park, a place for games, picnics and parties,

close to one of their two great artifical lakes. The surviving remains bear witness to these changing functions and this long history, stretching back well over a thousand years.

Historic monuments in Hillsborough (Belfast, 1977), DOE NI guide-card; Gaskell Brown, C, and Brannon, N F, 'The rath in Hillsborough Fort, Co Down', *Ulster J Archaeol* 41 (1978), 78-87; Baillie, M G L, *Tree-ring dating and archaeology* (London, 1982), 115-24.

32. BALLYCOPELAND WINDMILL   Co Down   J 579761

1.6 km west of Millisle on the B172 to Newtownards.

Since prehistoric times people have understood that grain produced by farmers has to be crushed into flour or meal before being suitable for consumption. This was done on a hand-operated grinding stone called a quern - a laborious and time-consuming operation. In Early Christian times manual querns were being replaced by mills which harnessed the natural power provided by fast-running water, so relieving people from this heavy work. By the 12th century in England there are documentary references to a further technological development - mills driven by windpower, but it does not seem that windmills were commonly introduced into Ireland until the 17th century.

Ballycopeland is the sole surviving example of a working windmill in Northern Ireland. This 'tower mill' may have been built at some time in the 1780s though an early 19th-century date is also possible, and it was worked until 1915 by sucessive generations of the McGilton family. For the next twenty years it lay idle until it was offered to the State by Mr Samuel McGilton. Some restoration work was carried out on the structure in the 1930s and 1950s but it was not until the 1970s that the mill was brought back to working order after a major programme of renovation. Worn and rotten iron and wooden parts were replaced and the sails were refurbished.

When the visitor stands outside the whitewashed stone tower the intricate internal arrangement of the mill

workings are hidden from the eye, but once inside the building the complexity of the mechanisms can be fully appreciated. The workings are not unlike those of a huge clock with each different part performing an important function necessary for the smooth working of the entire machine. A working scale model of the windmill is displayed in the miller's cottage which has been made into a small museum. It is useful for the visitor to view this model before proceeding to the windmill since it provides an understanding of how the mill worked. It also helps to illustrate how all the floor levels within the building interconnected with one another.

The range of buildings extending uphill from the carpark include the kiln-house and the miller's house. When grain arrived at the windmill its moisture content had to be reduced before it was ready to be ground. The sacks of grain would be taken from the cart and lifted through a trap-door to the first floor of the kiln-house (which was restored to its original working condition in 1991). There the grain would be tipped out onto the sloping floor made of steel plates. The heat produced by the kiln at ground floor level was directed by chimneys to the underside of the steel-plated floor and in this way the grain was dried. The dried grain was then re-sacked and taken to the windmill.

The cap of the windmill is mobile and the fantail (invented by Edmund Lee in England in 1745) moves the

Fig. 132 Ballycopeland Windmill, Co Down, in the 1950s before conservation.

sails into the face of the prevailing wind. When the sails of the windmill are set square into the wind the fantail lies in their shelter and remains at rest. If there is a change in wind direction the fantail is set in motion and this movement is transmitted through a series of iron gear wheels and shafts to the small wheels under the cap. The wheels are driven around and this turns the windshaft (on which the sails are hung) into the wind again. There are two doorways into the windmill. The west door is used when the sails are obstructing the main east door.

When the sails turn the power generated is transmitted through the windshaft and brake wheel to the wallower on the Hopper Floor, where its bevelled teeth engage with the brake wheel. The wallower drives the main shaft, which passes through the Stones Floor (where the grain is milled) down to the Drive Floor where it drives the great spur wheel. At Ballycopeland the main shaft appears to have been a reused ship's mast. Three cogs (called stone nuts) are powered on the Drive Floor from the great spur wheel. The cogs connect with and drive the three pairs of grinding stones situated above in the Stones Floor. The grinding stones are encased in wooden 'tuns'. The grain is raised by a hoist from the Ground Floor up to the Hopper Floor where it is poured into hoppers which guide it into the eyes of the stones. The resulting crushed grain then falls down chutes to the Ground Floor where it is sacked and taken away from the mill for consumption.

The 'tower mill' was the characteristic type of windmill in Ireland. Windmills proliferated particularly in the sheltered grain-growing areas of counties Down and Wexford. Over 100 windmills are recorded on the 1834

Ordnance Survey maps of Co Down, with a heavy concentration in the Ards peninsula. Water-mills were favoured elsewhere in Ulster and, outside Co Down, only some 20 windmills were in operation, with about half of this number in Co Armagh. Ballycopeland Windmill produced oatmeal and wheatmeal for human consumption, and a variety of crushed animal feedstuffs.

Ballycopeland Windmill is one of only a few industrial monuments in Northern Ireland which are in working order and can be visited by the public. It is a precious survival from the time before the invention of the internal combustion engine and the discovery of electricity. It forms a link with the long period when people depended on and exploited wind and water to provide power, so vital for the production of food in a grain-growing economy. The display in the miller's house takes us back even further, to the remote period when grinding with hand querns was the only known method. At Ballycopeland the main impression is one of change: changing technologies in the production of the most basic foodstuffs for people and animals.

Fig. 133 Cut-away drawing showing Ballycopeland Windmill's internal workings.

Green, E R R, *The industrial archaeology of County Down* (HMSO, Belfast, 1963), 5 and fig 3; McCutcheon, W A, *The industrial archaeology of Northern Ireland* (HMSO, Belfast, 1980), 227-31; *Ballycopeland Windmill* (Belfast, 1985), DOE NI guide-card.

FEATURE 14 UNDERWATER ARCHAEOLOGY

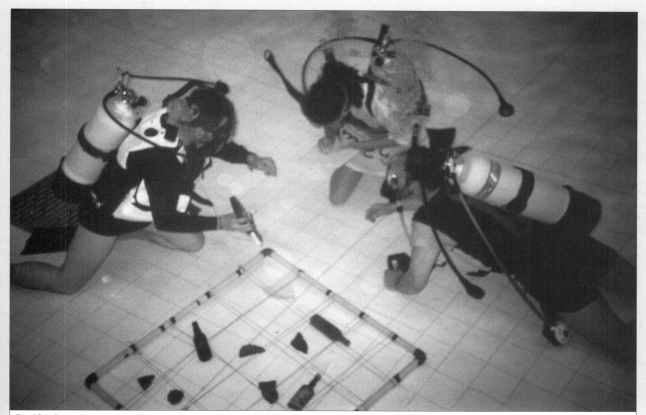

Fig. 134 Divers being trained in underwater surveying techniques (Colin Breen).

For centuries the people living in Ireland have relied on the sea for transport, trade, and communication. In addition, the sea provided food resources which could be exploited by coastal communities or traded with the inland population. While this maritime dependence is one which continues to the present, the social and economic monuments of past nautical activity are scattered along the coastline (harbours, light-houses and salt-pans) and on the sea-bed (shipwrecks). Historic monuments and archaeological discoveries on inland rivers and loughs - fishing weirs, dug-out canoes, bridges, crannogs - also testify to the importance of our waterways in former times. Since the sea and inland water-ways were clearly of great significance to our ancestors, it is surprising to discover that the archaeological investigation of our underwater heritage is a fairly recent development.

The story of underwater archaeology in Northern Ireland begins in 1968 when the Belgian underwater archaeologist Robert Sténuit led a team of French and Belgian divers on a two-season excavation of the *Girona*, a galleass of the Spanish Armada which sank near the Giant's Causeway on the north Antrim coast. Having taken part in the failed Spanish invasion of England in the summer of 1588, the ship had set out on its long homeward journey to Spain. Storm-battered and carrying the rescued crews from other ill-fated vessels, the *Girona* was on its way to sanctuary among the Catholic population of the west of Scotland when, on the dawn of 26 October 1588, she sank off Lacada Point during a terrible gale. While the location of the anchor, breechblocks, lead ingots (for the manufacture of small arms ammunition) and two bronze cannon on the ocean bed at or near the northern tip of Lacada Point indicated the likely resting-place of the *Girona*, no structural remains survived. The divers' work in the cold Atlantic waters did, however, recover a magnificent range of 16th-century material, from Renaissance jewellery and gold coins, to a wooden musket-stock and two astrolabes. The Ulster Museum successfully negotiated the acquisition of the materials recovered by the excavators, and the artefacts were put on display in 1972.

By the late 1980s there was a growing awareness that industrial and tourist activities were placing increased pressure on the underwater heritage and a number of initiatives were undertaken to counter the threats. The establishment in 1989 of the Irish Underwater Archaeological Research Team (IUART) brought archaeologists and government representatives from all over Ireland into partnership with the well-established sports diving community. With the aim of promoting underwater archaeology to a wider audience, the sports divers were taught archaeological techniques and procedures, while the archaeologists were introduced to the skills necessary for working under water. The result has been the creation of a well-equipped and trained body of people capable of undertaking excavations and surveys in underwater environments.

Two legal developments aided the growth of underwater archaeology in Northern Ireland. In 1992 the DOE NI became responsible for the protection of shipwrecks in Northern Ireland's territorial waters

Fig. 135 Selection of finds from the *Taymouth Castle* (Colin Breen).

under the Protection of Wrecks Act 1973 and in April 1993 the *Girona* was the first site to be designated as a historic wreck. The Historic Monuments and Archaeological Objects (NI) Order 1995 extended legal protection to all sites and objects located below the high-water mark and on the sea-bed. The Environment and Heritage Service was aware that in order to protect these sites it was necessary to compile a database, and so it funded the appointment of a Senior Research Fellow in the Institute of Irish Studies at Queen's University in 1993 to undertake the task of assembling a document-based record of shipwrecks along the coast of Northern Ireland. Colin Breen was appointed to carry out the work, and the Maritime Archaeological Project has now listed some 3000 wrecks and wreck-incidents, the majority of which date from the period after AD 1800. The next phase of the project will involve intensive sea-bed surveys to provide information on the precise location of shipwrecks.

In 1995 the first licensed underwater excavation of a shipwreck in Northern Ireland's territorial waters under the new legislation was undertaken off Cushendun on the east Antrim coast. The *Taymouth Castle*, a sailing ship built in Glasgow in 1865, had been travelling to Singapore with a cargo of ceramics, beer, spirits and building materials when she was caught in a violent gale on 3 January 1867 and was wrecked, with the loss of her entire crew, between Torr Head and Cushendun. The *Taymouth Castle* had been an experimental ship, incorporating an iron frame with wooden planking. The excavation revealed that the forward section (the bow) of the ship's iron framework lay intact on the sea-bed and a small portion of the outer hull was located nearby. An assemblage of Glasgow 'sponge ware' ceramics of mid 19th-century date was recovered, as well as beer and spirit bottles (still corked) and wooden packing-cases.

The Historic Monuments and Archaeological Objects (NI) Order

1995 also provides protection to sites and monuments located on the coastline below high-water mark - the inter-tidal zone. In 1995 and 1996 the Environment and Heritage Service was involved in a preliminary project which recorded a range of historic features in the inter-tidal zone on Strangford Lough in Co Down. An early harbour was identified at Nendrum (see Chapter 6) and a landing-place was investigated at Ringhaddy Castle, a tower-house of 15th-century date which had its upper levels rebuilt around 1600 (see also Chapter 9: Audley's Castle). The boulder foundations for a timber jetty were encountered on the fore-shore near to where a series of stone steps leads up to the castle. Similar landing-places have been identified at five other castle sites on Strangford Lough and Colin Breen points out that their coastal location would have provided the castle occupants with direct access to the contemporary sea-based communication network in medieval and post-medieval times. The fieldwork also identified a submerged Mesolithic woodland at Greyabbey Bay and a variety of 19th- and 20th-century ships and boats at Ringneill Quay, Castleward Bay and Quoile Quay. The remains of at least 15 fish-traps (artificial barriers of wood and stone designed to direct fish towards nets and baskets) of Early Christian and medieval date were discovered, emphasising the important role that fish played in the diet of the people who lived near the lough in past times.

Underwater work has also begun at sites on inland waterways and in inland loughs. At Inch Abbey (see Chapter 8) IUART divers recovered a number of worked timbers during

Fig. 136 Fish-trap in inter-tidal zone in Greyabbey Bay, Strangford Lough, Co Down.

the monitoring of a dredging scheme on the river Quoile in 1992. Also in 1992 Brian Williams led a team of IUART divers in survey work on the crannogs (see Chapter 7: Lough na Cranagh) of Lough Macnean in Co Fermanagh as part of the archaeological survey of the county and the two-week project was very successful. The dwelling area of a crannog lies above the surface of the lough, but its foundations lie under the water. The lake waters preserve organic materials used in construction and timbers from two crannogs were sampled for dating purposes. In addition, the divers discovered a wooden causeway leading from the lough-shore.

The important work currently being undertaken in Northern Ireland is already increasing our understanding and appreciation of our underwater heritage in what, until recently, was a neglected area of archaeology. As more sites are surveyed and excavated, in both coastal and inland waters, archaeo-logical perspectives on our past associations with the sea and internal waterways will advance and we will increasingly appreciate our underwater heritage.

Flanagan, L, *Girona* (Belfast, 1974); MacGrail, S, *Ancient boats in north-west Europe* (London, 1987); McCaughan, M, and Appleby, J, (ed) *The Irish Sea: aspects of maritime history* (Belfast, 1989); Dean, M, (ed) *Archaeology underwater: the Nautical Archaeological Society guide to principles and practice* (London, 1992); Boland, D, 'Underwater archaeology in Ireland', *Archaeology Ireland* 8.3 (1994), 13-14; Breen, C, 'The Taymouth Castle: the first shipwreck excavation in Northern Ireland', *Archaeology Ireland* 10.1 (1996), 30-1; Breen, C, 'Maritime archaeology in Northern Ireland: an interim statement', *International Journal of Nautical Archaeology* 25.1 (1996), 55-65; Williams, B, 'Intertidal archaeology in Strangford Lough', *Archaeology Ireland* 10.3 (1996), 14-16; O'Sullivan, A, McErlean, T, McConkey, R, and McCooey, P, 'Medieval fishtraps in Strangford Lough, Co Down', *Archaeology Ireland* 11.1 (1997), 36-8.

Appendices

LOCAL MUSEUMS AND HERITAGE CENTRES

GLOSSARY

including Feature 15:
Guide to the pronunciation of Irish words in the text
(prepared by Dr Kay Muhr)

READING LIST

INDEX

Fig. 137 Carrickfergus Castle, Co Antrim (Infra-red photograph by Tony Corey).

Local Museums and Heritage Centres

County Antrim

Carrickfergus Castle, Marine Highway, Carrickfergus.

Carrickfergus Gasworks, Irish Quarter West, Carrickfergus.

Causeway School Museum, Environment Resource Centre, 60 Causeway Road, Bushmills.

Dunluce Castle, Portrush.

Familia, The Ulster Heritage Centre, 64 Wellington Place, Belfast.

Giant's Causeway Centre, Giant's Causeway, Bushmills.

Lisburn Museum and Irish Linen Centre, Market Square, Lisburn.

Patterson's Spade Mill, Antrim Road, Templepatrick.

Ulster Museum, Botanic Gardens, Belfast.

County Armagh

Ardress House, Annaghmore, Portadown.

The Argory, Derrycaw Road, Moy, Dungannon.

Armagh County Museum, The Mall East, Armagh City.

Moneypenny's Lock, Horseshoe Lane, Brackagh, Portadown.

The Navan Centre, 81 Killylea Road, Armagh.

Palace Stables Heritage Centre, The Palace Demesne, Armagh City.

The Royal Irish Fusiliers Regimental Museum, Sovereign's House, The Mall, Armagh City.

Saint Patrick's Trian, English Street, Armagh City.

County Down

Ballycopeland Windmill, Millisle.

Burren Heritage Centre, 15 Bridge Road, Warrenpoint.

Castle Ward, Strangford.

Down County Museum, The Mall, Downpatrick.

Grey Abbey, Greyabbey.

Mount Stewart House and Gardens, Newtownards.

Nendrum Monastery, Mahee Island, Comber.

Newry Museum, Arts Centre, Bank Parade, Newry.

North Down Heritage Centre, Town Hall, Bangor Castle, Bangor.

Ulster Folk and Transport Museum, Cultra, Holywood.

County Fermanagh

Belleek Pottery Visitor Centre, Belleek.

Castle Coole, Enniskillen.

Crom Estate, Newtownbutler.

Devenish Island, Monastic Site.

Enniskillen Castle, Castle Barracks, Enniskillen.

Explorerne, Erne Gateway, Corry, Belleek.

Florence Court House, Florence Court.

Tully Castle, Tully.

County Londonderry

Amelia Earhart Cottage, Ballyarnett.

Foyle Valley Railway Centre, Foyle Road, Derry City.

Harbour Museum, Harbour Square, Derry City.

Hezlett House, Sea Road, Castlerock, Coleraine.

Springhill, Moneymore, Magherafelt.

The Tower Museum, Magazine Gate, Derry City.

County Tyrone

An Creggán – Creggan Visitor Centre, Creggan, Omagh.

Benburb Valley Heritage Centre, 89 Milltown Road, Tullymore Etra, Benburb.

Castlederg Visitor Centre, 26 Lower Strabane Road, Castlederg.

Cornmill Heritage Centre, Linenside, Coalisland.

Gray's Printing Press, Main Street, Strabane.

Sperrin Heritage Centre, 274 Glenelly Road, Cranagh.

Ulster-American Folk Park, Omagh.

Ulster History Park, Cullion, Lislap, Omagh.

Wellbrook Beetling Mill, Cookstown.

Further information on opening hours, admission costs, and exhibit contents can be found in the annual guide to Irish museums and heritage centres which is published in *Archaeology Ireland* each summer, or from the Northern Ireland Tourist Board.

Glossary

Angle bastion: A defensive projection on the wall of a fortification; see also *spear-shaped bastion*.

Annexe: A supplementary building.

Arcade: Two or more arches supported on piers or columns. Also a decorative motif carved in relief on a wall face (a blind arcade).

Barrel vault: A continuous vault, or stone roof, which is either semicircular or pointed in profile.

Bawn: A walled enclosure.

Bell-cote: A framework on a roof housing a bell.

Blanket bog: A bog formed through the growth of peat where natural drainage has been impeded, or where there has been a rise in the water-table.

Capital: The head of a column or *pilaster*.

Causeway: A raised road or walkway.

Chancel: The east part of a church where the main altar is usually reserved for the clergy and the choir.

Corbelling: A series of stone courses each built out over the one below, used to form a roof over a chamber.

Cornice: A projecting moulding set at the top of a wall or an arch.

Courtyard: A walled enclosure, usually surrounded by buildings and entered through a gateway.

Cremation: The practice of burning as a means of disposing of the dead.

Crow-stepped gable: Square steps on the coping of a gable wall.

Culvert: A covered drain which allows water to run underground.

Curtain wall: A defensive wall surrounding a castle or fortification.

Drystone walling: A form of masonry construction which does not involve the use of mortar. Stability is achieved through the skilful positioning of the stones.

Excarnation: The exposure of the dead to the elements to hasten decomposition.

Flanker, flanking tower: A defensive corner tower.

Gatehouse: A defensive building which protects a gateway.

Geophysical prospection: Non-destructive scientific prospection techniques which enable archaeologists to investigate the underlying physical properties of the earth at a site and detect features.

Gothick: The term applied to the 18th- and 19th-century revival of medieval gothic architectural features.

Hall: A principal room in a castle or great house where public events were held.

Inhumation: The practice of burial as a means of disposing of the dead.

Iron pan: A continuous, impermeable layer of iron in the soil.

Keep: A tower which acts as the central stronghold in a castle.

Machicolation: A projecting gallery, usually of stone, set at parapet level on the outside wall of a castle or tower-house, with an opening in its floor through which missiles can be dropped on enemies below. Usually protecting an entrance.

Megalith: A prehistoric tomb or structure made of large stones; from the Greek *mega* (large) and *lithos* (stone).

Nave: The western section of a church, where the lay people worshipped.

Palisade: A defensive wall of timber posts.

Pediment: A triangular gable, or a moulded triangular frame over an opening like a window for ornamental purposes.

Pilaster: A rectangular column projecting from a wall.

Rampart: A defensive stone wall or bank of earth, sometimes crowned with a *palisade*.

Revetment: A retaining wall, in *drystone walling*, of mortared stone, or of timber.

Ribbed vault: A vault carried on a framework of arched stone ribs designed to transfer the weight of the stone vault to the side walls or columns.

Roll moulding: A moulding of semicircular or more than semicircular section.

Rood screen: A screen separating the *nave* from the *chancel* in a church, on which a rood, or crucifix, was supported.

Shingles: Wooden tiles used for covering a roof.

Spear-shaped bastion: A projection set at an angle of a fortification which enabled a garrison to defend an extensive area with gun-fire.

String-course: A horizontal band of projecting stone which runs across a wall surface.

Tracery: The ornamental work in the head of a window made up of intersecting stone arches and geometrical shapes.

Transept: The transverse arms of a cross-shaped church. The north and south transepts meet at the junction of the *nave* and the *chancel*.

Ward: A castle *courtyard* or bailey.

Wattle: A wall made of interlaced wicker rods.

More detailed definitions of archaeological and architectural terminology can be found in the following books: Fleming, J, Honour, H, and Pevsner, N, *The Penguin Dictionary of Architecture*, third edition (Harmondsworth, 1980); Bray, W, and Trump, D, *The Penguin Dictionary of Archaeology*, second edition (Harmondsworth, 1982); Whitehouse, R, (ed), *The Macmillan Dictionary of Archaeology* (London, 1983); Jenner, M, *The Architectural Heritage of Britain and Ireland* (Harmondsworth, 1993).

FEATURE 15 | GUIDE TO THE PRONUNCIATION OF IRISH WORDS

Prepared by Dr Kay Muhr

(Department of Celtic, School of Medieval and Modern Languages, the Queen's University of Belfast)

All spellings are given in Classical/Early Modern Irish, with stress indicated by bold print. The symbol > is used to indicate where pronunciation changed at a later date.

Aedh Findliath	ay **fin**leea
aimhréidh	**av**ray
Airghialla	**air**-yeela
Alba	a**l**aba
Ard Macha	ard **ma**ha (> **wa**ha)
Bealach an Mhaighre	ballach an **wy**ra
Cathbhadh	**ka**hva
Cenél Conaill	kinal **konn**il
Cenél Eóghain	kinal **own**
Cladh Ruadh, an	an kly **rooa**
cloicthech	**klig**hach
Conchobhar	**kon**hover (> **konn**er)
Cnoc mBáine	kroc **maa**nya
Cú Chulainn	Koo **hull**in
Daimhinis	**dev**inish
Daire Lúráin	dirra **loor**ine
Deirdre	**der**dra
Doirse	**dir**sha
Dún Droma	doon **drum**a
Dún Ailinne	doon **alin**ya
Dún Eachdhach	doon **ech**ach
Dún Sobhairce	doon **sovark**ya (> **sork**ya)
Eamhain Mhacha	evin **va**ha (> awin **wa**ha)
an / i n-Eamhain	a **nev**in (> a **naw**in)
Inis Cúscraidh	inish **koo**skri
Leac na Rí	lyack na **ree**
Loch Gabhair	loch **gore**
Meadhbh	**mayv** (> **may-oo**)
ogham	**ohm**
Rechru	**rech**roo
Slighe Mhiodhluachra	shlee **vee**looachra
Sruthar	**shroo**har
Tuathal Teachtmhar	tooahal ty**acht**war
Uí Néill	ee **nyail**
Ulaidh	**ull**i

Reading List

General

M Aston, *Interpreting the landscape: landscape archaeology in local studies* (London, 1985).

J Bardon, *A history of Ulster* (Belfast, 1992).

A Brindley, *Irish prehistory: an introduction* (Dublin, 1995).

C Brady, M O'Dowd and B Walker (ed), *Ulster, an illustrated history* (London, 1989).

D A Chart (ed), *A preliminary survey of the ancient monuments of Northern Ireland* (HMSO, Belfast, 1940).

M Craig, *The architecture of Ireland* (London, 1982).

T Darvill, *Ancient monuments in the countryside*, English Heritage Archaeological Report No 5 (London, 1987).

E E Evans, *Prehistoric and Early Christian Ireland: a guide* (London, 1966).

A Hamlin and C Lynn (ed), *Pieces of the past* (HMSO, Belfast, 1988).

P Harbison, *Guide to the national and historic monuments of Ireland* (Dublin, 1992).

HMSO, *An archaeological survey of County Down* (HMSO, Belfast, 1966).

HMSO, *Historic monuments of Northern Ireland* (HMSO, Belfast, 1987).

J Hunter and I Ralston (ed), *Archaeological resource management in the UK: an introduction* (Stroud, 1993).

P Loughrey (ed), *The people of Ireland* (Belfast, 1988).

D Lowenthal and M Binney (ed), *Our past before us - why do we save it?* (London, 1981).

J P Mallory and T E McNeill, *The archaeology of Ulster* (Belfast, 1991).

F Mitchell and M Ryan, *Reading the Irish landscape*, third edition (Dublin, 1997).

F Mitchell, *Where has Ireland come from?* (Dublin, 1994).

S P Ó Ríordáin, *Antiquities of the Irish countryside* (revised 5th edition by R de Valera, London, 1979).

P Rahtz, *Invitation to archaeology* (Oxford, 1985).

C Renfrew and P Bahn, *Archaeology: theories, methods and practice* (London, 1991).

A Rowan, *The buildings of Ireland: north west Ulster* (Harmondsworth, 1979).

M Ryan (ed), *The illustrated archaeology of Ireland* (Dublin, 1991).

Prehistoric

R Bewley, *The English Heritage book of prehistoric settlements* (London, 1994).

R Bradley, *The social foundations of prehistoric Britain* (London, 1984).

G Cooney and E Grogan, *Irish prehistory: a social perspective* (Dublin, 1994).

P Harbison, *Pre-christian Ireland* (London, 1988).

M Herity and G Eogan, *Ireland in prehistory* (London, 1977).

R Hutton, *The pagan religions of the ancient British Isles* (London, 1991).

J V S Megaw and D D A Simpson, *Introduction to British prehistory* (Leicester, 1979).

M J O'Kelly, *Early Ireland* (Cambridge, 1989).

S Ó Nualláin, *Stone circles in Ireland* (Dublin, 1995).

M Parker-Pearson, *The English Heritage book of Bronze Age Britain* (London, 1993).

B Raftery, *Pagan Celtic Ireland* (London, 1994).

E Shee Twohig, *Irish megalithic tombs* (Shire Archaeology 63, 1990).

Early Christian

C Bourke, *Patrick: the archaeology of a saint* (HMSO, Belfast, 1993).

F J Byrne, *Irish kings and high kings* (London, 1973).

N Edwards, *The archaeology of early medieval Ireland* (London, 1990).

A Hamlin, 'The early Irish church: problems of identification',
The early church in Wales and the west, ed N Edwards and A Lane (Oxford, 1992), 138-44.

K Hughes and A Hamlin, *The modern traveller to the early Irish church*, second edition (Dublin 1997).

H G Leask, *Irish chuches and monastic buildings: volume one* (Dundalk, 1955).

C Manning, *Early Irish monasteries* (Dublin, 1995).

D Ó Cróinín, *Early medieval Ireland, 400 - 1200* (Harlow, 1995).

M and L de Paor, *Early Christian Ireland* (London, 1958).

N Patterson, *Cattle lords and clansmen: the social structure of early Ireland* (Notre Dame, 1994).

Medieval

T B Barry, *The archaeology of medieval Ireland* (London, 1987).

J Bradley, *Walled towns in Ireland* (Dublin, 1995).

A Gwynn and R N Hadcock, *Medieval religious houses: Ireland* (Blackrock, 1970).

H G Leask, *Irish castles* (revised second edition reprint, Dundalk, 1951).

H G Leask, *Irish churches and monastic buildings: volumes two and three* (Dundalk, 1960).

T E McNeill, *Anglo-Norman Ulster: the history and archaeology of an Irish barony, 1177-1400* (Edinburgh, 1980).

T E McNeill, *The English Heritage book of castles* (London, 1992).

M Richter, *Medieval Ireland: the enduring tradition* (Dublin, 1988).

R Stalley, *The Cistercian monasteries of Ireland* (London, 1987).

D Sweetman, *Irish castles and fortified houses* (Dublin, 1995).

Plantation and Later

M Bence-Jones, *A guide to Irish country houses* (revised edition, London, 1988).

C Brady and R Gillespie (ed), *Natives and newcomers: the making of Irish colonial society, 1534-1641* (Suffolk, 1986).

D Crossley, *Post-medieval archaeology in Britain* (Leicester, 1990).

G Camblin, *The town in Ulster* (Belfast, 1951).

C E Orser, Jr and B M Fagan, *Historical archaeology* (New York, 1995).

A Gailey, *Rural houses of the north of Ireland* (Edinburgh, 1984).

R Gillespie, *Colonial Ulster: the settlement of east Ulster, 1600-1641* (Cork, 1985)

R Gillespie, 'Plantations in early modern Ireland', *History Ireland* 1.4 (1993), 43-7.

E R R Green, *The industrial archaeology of County Down* (HMSO, Belfast, 1963).

F Hamond, *Antrim coast and glens industrial heritage* (HMSO, Belfast, 1991).

G A Hayes-McCoy, *Ulster and other Irish maps c.1600* (Dublin, 1964).

P M Kerrigan, *Castles and fortifications in Ireland, 1485-1945* (Cork, 1995).

W A McCutcheon, *The industrial archaeology of Northern Ireland* (HMSO, Belfast, 1980).

P Robinson, *The Plantation of Ulster* (Dublin, 1984).

A major source of information for all those interested in recent archaeological activity is the collection of summary excavation reports published annually in *Excavations: Summary Accounts of Archaeological Excavations in Ireland*. The quarterly magazine *Archaeology Ireland* provides a colourful overview of recent discoveries, new research, forthcoming events, and publication reviews. In addition, the pages of the quarterly magazine *History Ireland* contain many articles on aspects of Early Christian, medieval and early modern Ireland.

The Institute of Irish Studies at the Queen's University of Belfast is currently engaged in the publication of the *Ordnance Survey Memoirs of Ireland*. The Memoirs were compiled during the 1830s and provide detailed information on life in Ireland in the period prior to the Great Famine, documenting the topography, population, buildings, antiquities, and religious, social and economic activities parish by parish.

The Northern Ireland Place-Names Project is situated within the Department of Celtic at the School of Medieval and Modern Languages, the Queen's University of Belfast. A large database has been compiled of the original (usually Irish) form and meaning of place-names from all over Northern Ireland. Seven volumes of place-names from counties Antrim, Down and Londonderry have been published in conjunction with the Institute of Irish Studies, the Queen's University of Belfast.

Detailed reports of most of Ulster's archaeological excavations have appeared in the *Ulster Journal of Archaeology*, first published in 1853 and now in its third series. It is published by the Ulster Archaeological Society.

Index